From Joe & Moira Walsh.

KIELDER

Country Walks

Other *Questa* guides, published and in production

Walks with Children in the Lake District:
Patterdale
Buttermere and the Vale of Lorton
Borrowdale
Around Coniston

Walks with Children in the Surrey Hills
Walks with Children in the South Downs
Walks with Children in the Yorkshire Dales

Brontë Country Walks
Country Walks around Keswick

KIELDER

Country Walks

Alan Hall

A Questa Guide

Q

ISBN 1 898808 04 X

Questa Publishing
27 Camwood, Clayton Green, Bamber Bridge
PRESTON, Lancashire, PR5 8LA

ADVICE TO READERS

Readers are advised that while the author has taken every effort to ensure the accuracy of this guidebook, and has been required to revisit all the routes during the course of preparing the book, changes can occur which may affect the contents.

The publishers would welcome notes of any changes that you find, but neither the publisher nor the author can accept responsibility for errors or omissions, or for any loss or injury howsoever caused.

Any reference to a path or other lines of ascent does not imply that a right of way exists.

This book has been compiled in accordance with the *Guidelines for Writers of Path Guides* published by the Outdoor Writers' Guild.

Also by Alan Hall

The Border Country

Border Pubs & Inns: A Walker's Guide

Printed by
Carnmor Print and Design, London Road, Preston

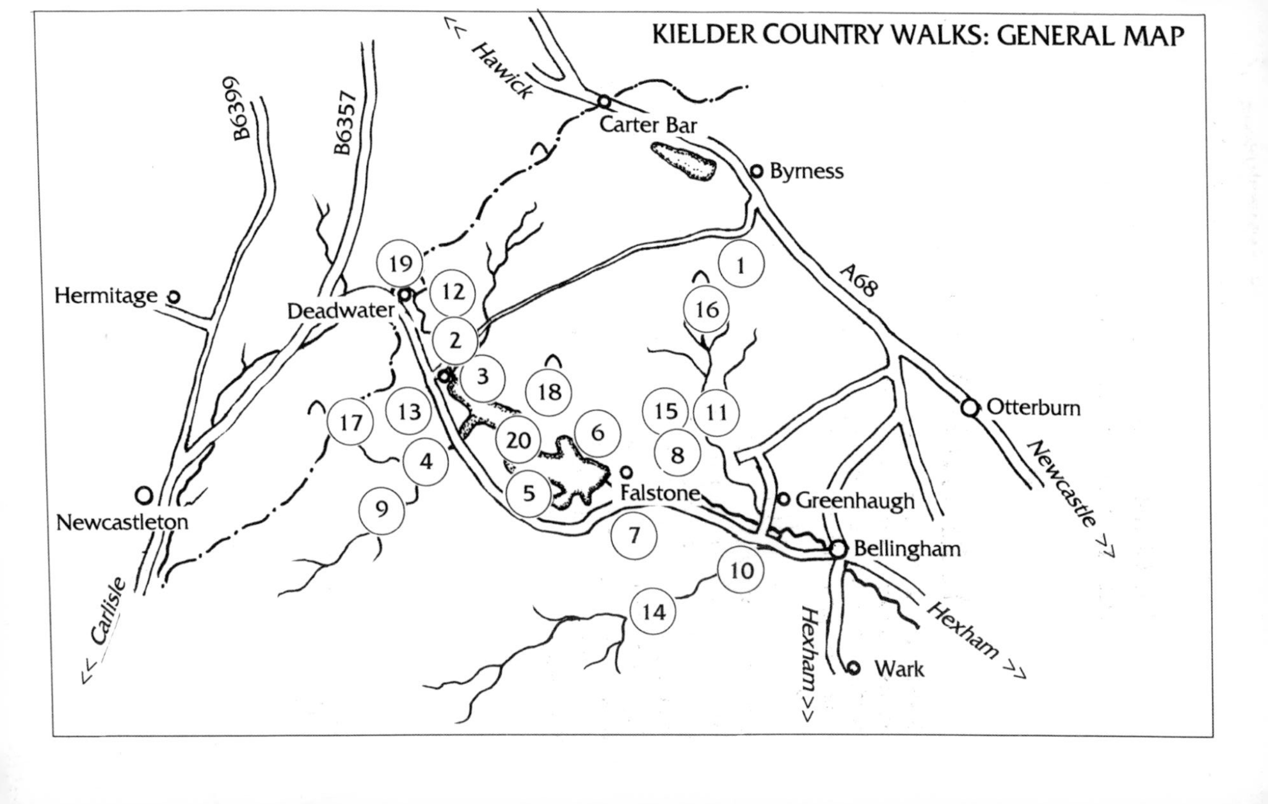
KIELDER COUNTRY WALKS: GENERAL MAP
<< Hawick
Carter Bar
Byrness
A68
Otterburn
Newcastle >>
B6399
B6357
Hermitage
Deadwater
Newcastleton
<< Carlisle
Falstone
Greenhaugh
Bellingham
Hexham >>
Hexham >>
Wark
1
2
3
4
5
6
7
8
9
10
11
12
13
14
15
16
17
18
19
20

To Christopher, Catriona, Chloe,
and the twins Sophie and Natalie.

Acknowledgements

Grateful thanks to all who lightened my step with encouraging words and expert knowledge on this ever-changing corner of the Borderland. With your help, may I through this small volume assist others to appreciate and enjoy this countryside you love and call Kielder.

To Chris Probert, Bill Burlton and Mike Sanderson of Forest Enterprise, Forestry Commission; to Chris Pringle of Northumbrian Water, to Catriona Mulligan of the Northumbrian National Park, to John McErlane, Rights of Way Officer, and Pat Morse, Kielder Castle Visitor Centre. Last but not least to James Hall of Deadwater and Edgar Charlton of Whitchester whose goat watch and handed-down tales of generations past have taken me just that little bit further along the path to understanding the land and life of Tynedale.

All photographs and maps relating to Kielder are by the author.

CONTENTS

INTRODUCTION

"On Kielder side the wind blaws wide
There sounds nae hunting horn
That rings sae sweet as the winds that beat
'Round banks where Tyne is born".

A Jacobite's Exile: Swinburne

KIELDER: PAST AND PRESENT

The area covered in this guide, known simply as "Kielder", contains North Tynedale and its surrounding hills, stretching from Bellingham to the Scottish Border, where it is restrained by the bastions of Peel and Carter Fells.

Contradictory Kielder, said to mean either, "violent stream" or "flat wet area", continues to confuse orthographers. Thomas Musgrave, Captain of Bewcastle started it all in 1578 with "Kelder", local scribes then used "Keelder", which was changed in 1775 by the Duke of Northumberland when "Keilder" Castle was built. In 1862 the Ordnance Survey introduced "Kielder", and so it has remained, apart from a temporary blip when the North British Railway entered it in railway records as "Kieldar".

Millions of years and much traumatised strata have gone to form this quilted mass of gently-folding hills on which we walk today. To the south, sandstone and limestone ridges running east-west are broken by eroded depressions; to the north less tilting of base rock resulted in more elongated hills of fell sandstone, such as Carter Fell and Peel Fell.

The Ice Age, some 12,000 years ago, finally fashioned the area. Glaciers flowed east into the southern sections slowly eroding the soft shales, while an ice cap sat on the higher ground to the north, rounding the northern hills. Ultimately, the ice retreated, depositing powdered rock or "till" over the underlying rock, resulting in vast areas of bog.

Today these saturated peat bogs in periods of prolonged rain overflow, turning the many burns of Kielder into raging peat-stained cascades. Evidence of these flash floods can be seen in the huge water-worn rocks deposited in Lewis Burn and Kielder Burn.

After the ice, much of upper Tynedale, including the higher fells, lay beneath a canopy of alder, oak and birch, with the valley floor a wet and inhospitable place. Then came man, followed by his sheep, who between them cleared the area of its sylvan cloak, and it is now only by burn and cleugh that the indigenous alder and birch remain.

Thus was this wilderness created, a land visited and occasionally settled through the centuries by Stone, Bronze and Iron Age man, Roman, Anglo-Saxon, Norse and Dane, Pict and Scot, who fashioned a remote and wild dale with a "frontier feel". This frontier feel was described as "lean, hungry and waste", and from the 13th to the 17th century was much given to feuding, reiving and sheep; then in the last two centuries to the mining of hard-won coal, iron ore and limestone. Indeed, when Stephen Oliver was rambling around Northumberland in the early 1830s there was no cart track to Kielder, and it was not until the mid 1800s that a road found its way through Deadwater into Scotland.

Now with one market town, few villages and very few people, this land of space, fresh air and an independent spirit, has returned to peace and solitude. A land much loved by those who have reason or resources to visit, though largely unknown by the majority.

THE APPEAL OF KIELDER

The Kielder scene has swung full circle, its fells and valleys once more overlade with trees and submerged by water. Time, the great healer, has softened this sudden change caused by the serried ranks of countless conifers and the intrusion of reservoirs, presenting now a pleasing prospect of mature trees and settled water with many varying habitats. Forest Enterprise are replanning and restructuring the 40,000 hectares of Kielder Forest, thus encouraging and providing facilities for wildlife and visitors. So also Northumbrian Water, with its varied waterside facilities at Tower Knowe and Leaplish, and Northumberland National Park, an authority devoted to conservation and duty bound to provide facilities for the visitor. Couple this enthusiasm for their tenancy with the history-soaked isolation of Tynedale and all lovers of the outdoors have an invitation that cannot be ignored.

For the walker there are scenic routes to please and challenge. Family adventures for the young and young at heart, longer rambles by quiet places, plus a day's hike on the high hills or a marathon circuit of Kielder Water. By forest, fell and waterside, where ghosts of the past and whispering solitude walk hand in hand with the visitor. That's "Kielder Appeal".

FAUNA AND FLORA OF KIELDER

FAUNA: Kielder is a delight for the zoologist, and paradise for the ornithologist, with April to early June providing the most interest. In the forest, dappled roe deer and red-tailed fox live alongside stoats and weasels. Raptors (birds of prey with curved beaks and claws), graceful in flight, lethal in intent, provide occasional sightings; look out for the goshawk. Beneath the forest canopy insect feeders abound, chaffinches, woodpeckers and coal tits, with wrens and robins below; all no doubt appreciative of the many nest boxes. After the thinning stage larger birds such as woodcock, pigeon and thrush appear, with the great grey shrike a regular winter visitor. Adders, though shy, can often be seen; our largest snake's bite is rarely fatal, but is best avoided.

On the open fell, small herds of fine-horned feral goats graze the heather-clad Cheviots; roe deer inhabit the cleughs and moorland fringes with foxes, mountain hares, stoats and weasels. Hen harriers, merlins, falcons, kestrels and owls represent the raptors, with red grouse, curlew, snipe and tumbling plover frequent companions for the walker. Of the smaller birds meadow pipits and skylarks are the most numerous.

By waterside, complimenting Kielder's fine burns and mature reservoirs, the wildlife is outstanding and easy to observe. The majority of birds are migratory, and range from the regal osprey and goosander to the tiny, bobbing dipper. Stately herons, flashing kingfishers, swans, geese, dabbling and diving duck, moorhen, waterhen, coot, grebes, gulls, terns, sandpiper and wagtails are present in this colourful community. Otters, though not in any numbers, can be seen, and feral mink now inhabits all waterways. Badger sets are also in evidence here and there.

Insects are legion, colourful butterflies and dragonflies, pond skaters and beetles to the largest sawflies in Britain. Like most northern forests and waterways, Kielder has its share of biting and stinging insects, the most voracious of these "nasties" being the female midge and horseflies who attack the unprepared in humid, warm and windless conditions in summer. Always carry an insect repellent (containing Diethyltoluamide - 'Diet' for short) to avoid an irritating experience.

FLORA: On the hills and ridges colourful heathers reign supreme, with sphagnum moss and its cousins on the bogs and mires, flanked by white cotton grass (Scotsman's heids). Patches of sticky sundew, bog asphodel, crowberry, cloudberry, blaeberry and bog rosemary can be seen on Larriston Fell and Three Pikes. Of the grasses that wave on the high fells, molinia (purple moor grass/flying bent) predominates; on the lower slopes bracken threatens, while by the limestone outcrops fine grasses co-exist with thyme, rock rose and plantain.

At lower levels primrose, vetch and tormentil brighten up the walk, as do shy orchids on the wetter pastures and plateaux.

The forest is composed mainly of Sitka spruce on the higher slopes, and Norway spruce. On heathery ground pines are preferred, the native Scots pine on the drier knowes and lodgepole pines on the deep peat areas. Stands now often contain larch, for its pleasing colours, and are fringed with rowan, silver birch, alder and ash. By rivers and pastures stately ash, oak, sycamore, chestnut and beech stand supreme.

Silviculture and forest management techniques have changed dramatically over the last thirty years, stands are now left unthinned to be clear harvested after about forty-five years. Couple that with the introduction of the chainsaw in the 1960s together with motorised timber extraction, the development of sophisticated harvesting machinery during the 1970s and 1980s, and we have today's labour force of around 300 managing Britain's largest forest. A forest producing 400,000 cubic metres annually for newsprint and paper making, particleboard, the construction industry, the packaging and pallet industry and, of course, Christmas trees. Recent discussions regarding the use of Kielder timber have included brash and branches as a fuel source for a power station.

KIELDER'S ACCESS, ACCOMMODATION AND AMENITIES

Access by Air: International and internal airports at Newcastle and Edinburgh.

Rail: Inter City services: the east coast line, stopping at Newcastle-upon-Tyne and Berwick-upon-Tweed; the west coast line at Carlisle.

Road: Regardless of direction every approach to North Tynedale and Kielder is a scenic route, pleasing the eye and exciting the appetite. Two trunk roads, A68(T) from Jedburgh to Otterburn and A696(T) from Newcastle-upon-Tyne to Otterburn, approach Kielder. Access to Bellingham, from Otterburn is via B6320; from Corbridge the A68 and a minor road via Redesmouth; from Hexham the B6320. To Kielder village, the B6357 to Saughtree and a narrow road with passing places to Kielder.

Internal roads: West from Bellingham to Kielder Water dam on a minor road, from where the C200 whisks wheeled vehicles alongside Kielder Water to Kielder village. Country lanes connect the few hamlets and outlying farms. A narrow Forest Drive, with passing places and a toll, rattles north east from Kielder castle for 12 miles/19.2 km over Blakehope Nick (at 1481ft/451m the highest road summit on the Border) to the A68(T) at Blakehopeburnhaugh. The roads are well served with car parks, viewpoints, picnic places and toilets.

Accommodation: is available throughout Kielder - hotels, inns, guest houses, bed and breakfast (including farm house), self-catering, caravan and camp sites, youth hostel plus 18 backpacking forest sites. The majority are centred in and around Bellingham, Kielder village and Falstone. Details are available from Bellingham Tourist Information Centre and the visitor centres at Kielder Castle, Tower Knowe and Leaplish Waterside Park.

Amenities: Kielder Castle Visitor Centre, suitable for disabled visitors, with audio visual display of forest life, art gallery, café, gift shop (including guidebooks, maps, outdoor equipment etc), plus cycle hire.

Tower Knowe Visitor Centre, information centre, restaurant, gift shop (guidebooks, maps etc), audio visual exhibition, ferry bookings, evening cruises and landrover safaris.

Leaplish Waterside Park, information, restaurant, gift shop, cycle, horse, canoe, sailboard, and boat hire plus instruction, landrover safaris, fishing permits and the time clock for KWCCW.

Hawkhope, car park, picnic benches, toilets and cycle hire.

Activities: Forest, fell and waterside walks, guided walks, nature trails, orienteering, adventure playgrounds, family camping, mountain bike and horse riding routes.

Water activities: ferry cruises, sailing, water ski, canoe, sailboard, burn and reservoir fishing.

Activity holidays with accommodation: Calvert Trust, Kielder Water, water and land-based adventure holidays for the disabled.

Hawkhirst Adventure Camp, Kielder Water, water and land-based activities for youth groups etc.

MAKING THE MOST OF THE GUIDE

Maps:
OS Map: Landranger Sheet 80, The Cheviot Hills, 1:50000
OS Map: Explorer 1, Kielder Water, 1:25000

Aims: To introduce Kielder to all walkers, enabling them to explore with enthusiasm and enjoyment. Twenty walks of high interest and scenic appeal are included.

Chapter 1: Forest Fringes and Waterside Trails: Easy and Pleasing.
Chapter 2: Adventurous Rambles: With the Curlew's Cry.
Chapter 3: Through Forest to Fell: Where Eagles Fly.

Layout: Each chapter is introduced with a portrait of the landscape and a thumb-nail description of the walks.

Each walk, with a map, Graded 1 (short and waymarked) to 4 (long and high, often over unmarked fell) is then described in detail - length, time, grade, highlights etc, followed by a step-by-step account of the route. Items of interest (for no walk is complete without them) are sprinkled throughout the route description.

The photographs portray Kielder as the author saw it, including general views and specific shots of individual walks.

A Glossary of local names and words is followed by a Bibliography and applicable Useful Information.

Distances and Ascent: All distances and ascent have been carefully measured, and then rounded up or down. For shorter distances, no distinction has been made between yards and metres, both being approximate.

KEY TO MAPS

➔	START of walk
.-·-.	Border Line
□	Village or township
▭	Farm or house
	Road
======	Forest road/Farm track
-●--●-	Route/Footpath
→	Direction marker
++++++	Former railway
	Reservoir
	River
	Burn/Stream
=	Bridge
⌒	Summit of hill
	Cairn/Currick
	Crags
O	Cave
	Quarry
☼	Ancient settlement
◌	Druid's Circle
✝	Church/Burial Ground
	Castle
	Pele Tower/ Bastle
	Fire/Audio Tower
	Woodland - Conifer
	Woodland - Broad-leaved
P	Car Park
	Picnic Place
	Camp Site
	Viewpoint

WALKING IN KIELDER

Overhead: Kielder was once described as "cool, wet and windy", based no doubt on the premise that it was too far north to be warm, too far west to be dry, and too far east to be calm. For an upland area the precipitation is relatively low, averaging 50-55 inches per year, less than half the annual deluge experienced on upland areas in the west. Severe snow storms and sustained winter frosts are a rare occurrence, as are wind speeds in excess of 50 mph. Meteorological records show May, June and July as "warm, dry and calm" with long hours of daylight.

Underfoot: The majority of low level and middle distance walks cover waymarked paths, forest roads and paths, grassy bridleways and disused railtracks. Likewise the high level walks, though they also include, just for a change, sections of untracked fell and bible black hags with Kielder Water Challenge Circuit occasionally testing your resolve with tussocks, brash and overgrown stumps.

Equipment: The choice is simple and effective; clothes and footwear to cope with conditions overhead and underfoot - warm and dry in winter, cool and comfortable in summer, paying attention to the most severe conditions likely to be encountered. For a full day always carry map and compass (with the ability to use both), water and emergency rations, a first aid kit, torch and whistle.

Safety: Knowledge of your surroundings and of yourself is the greatest aid to safety. Always inform someone of your route and "Heed Well the Placement of your Feet". Simple rules apply should you sustain an injury - a basic knowledge of first aid - a knowledge of the rescue procedure (Tel: 999 Police, for the Mountain Rescue Team). If alone and immobilised use the International Rescue Signal - six long blasts on a whistle, torch or voice, repeated at one minute intervals; the acknowledging reply - three short blasts. And always stay put until help arrives, locating a moving casualty can be hazardous and time consuming.

Kielder Codes

GUARD against all risk of fire
PROTECT trees, plants and wildlife

LEAVE no litter; and things as you find them, take nothing away
KEEP dogs and animals under proper control
LEAVE dogs at home during LAMBING TIME - April-May
AVOID damaging buildings, fences, hedges, walls and signs
RESPECT the work of the forest and the countryside
OBSERVE all signs, do not leave open or obstruct gates
PLEASE RESPECT the peace and quiet of Kielder

FOREST ENTERPRISE CUSTOMER CARE STATEMENT

1) Monitor all recreation facilities and services in Kielder Forest on a regular basis.
2) Aim to maintain our facilities and services at consistently high standards.
3) Investigate any reported fault/complaint, undertake any necessary remedial action.
4) Do our utmost to ensure that our facilities are open at the times advertised.

WE WOULD ASK YOU OUR VISITORS TO:

1) Obey all warning notices, forest operations such as tree felling take place throughout the forest all year round.
2) Take advantage of waymarked trails for walking, cycling and horse-riding, they have been chosen because they provide good views and easy access into the forest.
3) Park sensibly and do not obstruct barriers or other access points.
4) Do everything you can to avoid disturbing wildlife.
5) Respect all users of the forest, Kielder has many visitors who engage in a wide variety of recreational pursuits.
6) Please let us know if you have any complaints or comments. You can let us know through the visitors' book at Kielder Castle or Kielder camp site, or by contacting the Environmental Officer - address and telephone in Useful Information.

NORTHUMBERLAND NATIONAL PARK
"Make the Most of your Visit"

In addition to the Curlew Country Code, the leaflet carries helpful advice on - Rights of Way, colour coded Yellow - footpaths, Blue - bridleways and Red - Byways; The Environment, Safety and Organised Activities, within the confines of the Park.

CHAPTER 1

FOREST FRINGES & WATERSIDE TRAILS: Easy and Pleasing

An All-Seasons selection of short yet rewarding trails of discovery for the family, the beginner and the young at heart. Achievable walks, peppered with items of interest along the way, open up the exciting new world of Kielder. Each walk has been chosen for its scenic delights and character that typifies the many facets of forest and waterside fringes, giving every visitor a full menu of Kielder delights, that will encourage a return visit to this little-known gem in the Northumbrian Borders.

Each trail is circular with car parking and picnic areas at the start, together with maps of the route and explanatory notes. In many cases toilet facilities and a Visitor Centre are at hand or nearby, as at Kielder Castle or Leaplish Waterside Park. For the less nimble there is a circular section of The Duke's Trail designed for wheel chairs and push chairs in addition to several linear routes on sections of other walks: where appropriate these are mentioned in the text.

The trails, with their viewpoints and interest boards, are on waymarked paths and tracks. Forest Enterprise walks follow the "two tree" symbol, while Northumbrian Water walks pursue an orange arrowhead along prepared paths on grass or pine needles. All the routes are distinct and nowhere difficult, zigzagged or stepped for easy ascent or descent, and can be comfortably and safely completed in trainers, although waterproof footwear is recommended in winter.

Finally, may I suggest to the enthusiast that these short walks are too good to be dismissed or neglected on account of their length and apparent lack of challenge. String a few together by utilising a common starting point, use a car, or better still MV Osprey (Kielder Water ferry) to get from walk to walk. These walks are fun.

Further walks are listed in Border Forest Park Guide Map and Kielder Water Self-Guided Trails.

FAMILY WALKS - At a Glance

By Blakehopeburnhaugh on Kielder's fringe by the A68(T), Walk 1 leaves the Forest Drive for a spot of sylvan gorge walking to the tumbling delights of Hindhope Linn. Walk 2, from Kielder Castle Visitor Centre, combines the informative Duke's Trail with the woodland pleasures of the Duchess Trail, whilst Walk 3 follows the Border Counties railbed and Kielder Viaduct to a Bronze Age burial cairn, returning by the shores of Bakethin reservoir.

Walk 4 follows two of Kielder's finest burns as it treads the old coal toll road. Walks 5 & 6 see charismatic Kielder Water from both sides, exploring man's mark, ancient and modern, Walk 5 begins from the scenically inviting Bull Crag, while Walk 6 winds along the wooded shore to the winsome peninsula of The Belling.

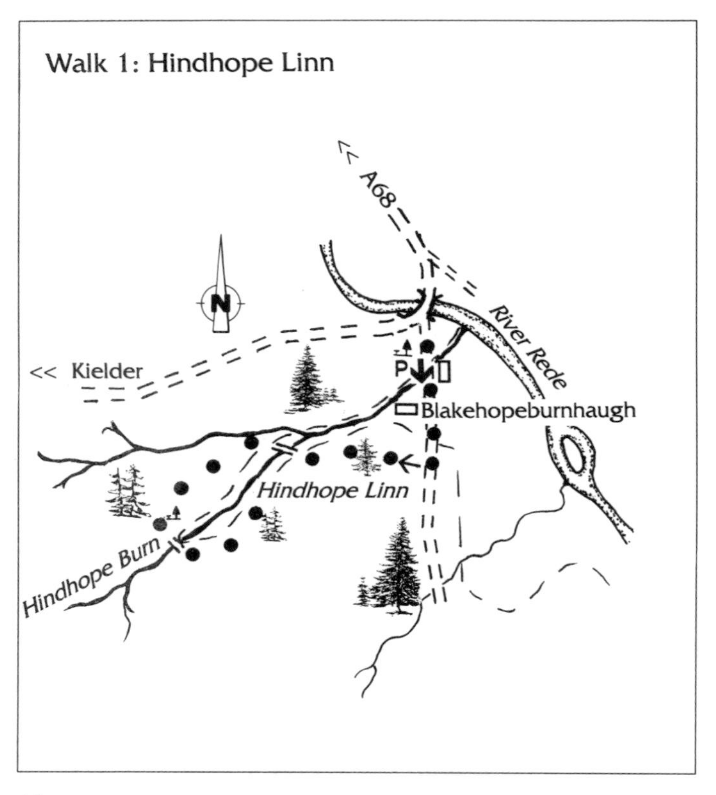

WALK 1:
HINDHOPE LINN

Blakehopeburnhaugh Picnic Place - Hindhope Burn - Hindhope Linn - Blakehopeburnhaugh Picnic Place.

Start/Finish: Blakehopeburnhaugh Car Park (GR.784002) 2 miles/3.2 km south from Byrness and ½ mile/0.8 km south of the A68(T) at the eastern end of Forest Drive.

Type of walk: *A short walk of 1¼ miles/2 km to the pencil thin linn of Hindhope, one of the many secret places deep within Kielder's numerous tree-lined gorges. Ascending a mere 115ft/35m, this walk, on waymarked paths, is a fine introduction to the hidden delights of the forest. Wear practical footwear and clothing, take your camera and see how many wild flowers you can identify.*

Accommodation and refreshments: Kielder and Byrness: Bed & Breakfast at Blakehopeburnhaugh Farm.

THE WALK: From the car park/picnic area close by the Forest Drive, a signposted scenic toll road from the A68(T) to Kielder, and a short cut to/from Upper North Tynedale, walk south on the Pennine Way/ forest road, directed by yellow arrowhead waymarks, pass the farmhouse flowers of Blakehopeburnhaugh to the west.

In the local vernacular, Blake - a common place name, hope - a sheltered valley, burn - a hill stream, haugh - flat riverside field, all add up to the longest name on the 270 miles/432 km of the Pennine Way.

As the conifers creep close to the roadside turn right, i.e. west, on a waymarked path through an open and airy stand of Scots pine, the only indigenous conifer in Kielder, high above a half-hidden gorge festooned with a pleasing mix of sun-shafted vegetation. This picturesque path swings left before descending, via steps, to Hindhope Burn and the delightful sound and sight of the cascade of Hindhope Linn. The word "linn", Scottish for waterfall, is a reminder that centuries ago this land was part of Scotland.

Returning from the linn ascend the left bank of the gorge on a stepped path and continue south-west above the burn and tumbling linn, overshadowed by Douglas fir, for ¼ mile/250m to meet a welcoming picnic bench. The path then crosses a footbridge and the return path is north-east through a pleasing mix of well spaced timber to join the outward path above the waterfall. Return via the venerable Scots pine to Blakehopeburnhaugh, farm, car park and picnic place.

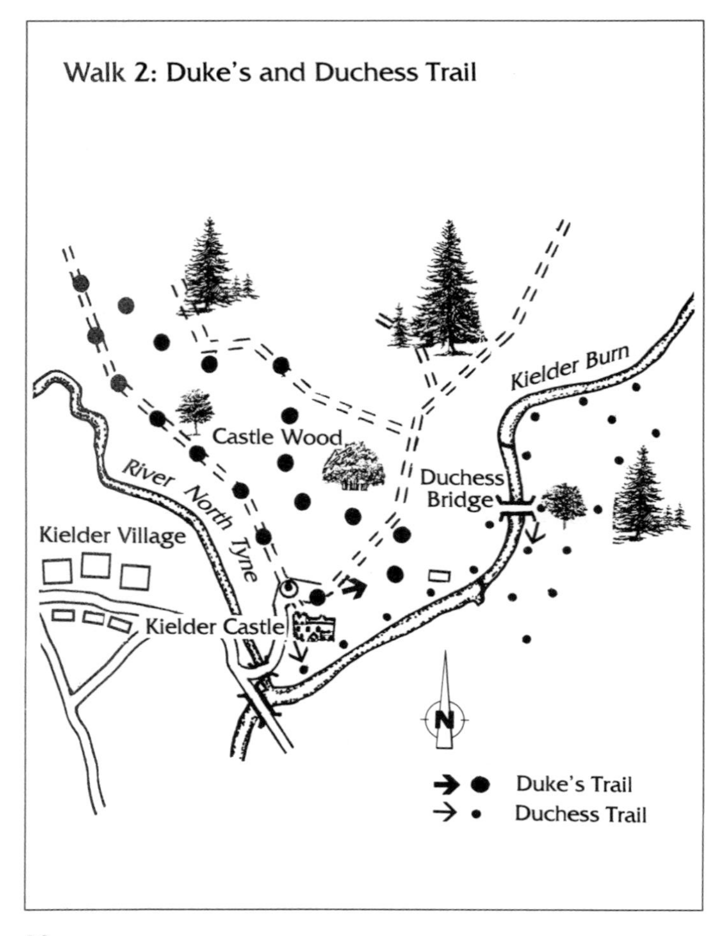

WALK 2:
DUKE'S & DUCHESS TRAIL

Kielder Castle - The Well - Castle Wood - Ravenshill Wood - Visitor Centre - Kielder Burn - Duchess Bridge - Jamie's Crags - Kielder Burn - Kielder Castle.

Start/Finish: Kielder Castle Visitor Centre (GR.633935) above Kielder village. Parking at Castle Wood.

Type of walk: *The two walks, Grade 1, can be combined to form a figure of eight journey of 3½ miles/5.6 km, or done as two singles of 1¾ miles/2.8 km. Easy on the eye and feet, both waymarked walks are mines of information, with the Duchess trail a particular delight, by burn and packhorse bridge winding through an ever-changing canopy. Rich in flora and fauna with birdsong from start to finish, the combined walks on constructed paths and grassy tracks take in the region of 2½ hours.*

A shortened Duke's Trail for wheelchairs and pushchairs, from Kielder Castle, circles the adventure play area before ascending to Castle Hill on a route full of interest and information.

Accommodation and refreshments: in nearby Kielder.

Completed in 1775 by Newton of Newcastle for the Duke of Northumberland, Kielder Castle, an imposing castellated shooting lodge is reputed to have cost £1,313-4s-3d. It was purchased by the Forestry Commission in 1930 and is now an imposing Visitor Centre.

The Duke's Trail: The waymarked Duke's Trail begins, and exits on to Forest Drive, descending east through trees to the play area before ascending via the castle viewing point, the pond and the arboretum to Castle Hill. This is a section of particular interest and information, keep an eye out for the informative wooden plaques, and carvings of the occupants of the forest.

After a zigzag in the path, cross Forest Drive and enter Castle Wood on a thin but distinct grassy path before swinging right, i.e. north, to the edge of a clearing to join the wide forest road. This wood and the oncoming Ravenshill Wood are a pleasing mix of ancient and modern woodland, much appreciated by the chattering chaffinches and drilling woodpeckers.

Turn left, i.e. west, beyond the clearing, before swinging on to a waymarked path into Ravenshill Wood. Continue for ¼ mile/400m, to a sharp left turn on the road leading back, by Ravenshill Riding Centre and Kielder campsite, to Kielder Castle.

The Duchess Trail: Also waymarked, the Duchess Trail descends south from Kielder Castle to Kielder Burn, and pursues a picturesque route north-east, by burbling burn and meadow, for 700 yds/m to the packhorse bridge known as the Duchess Brig.

Jane, second Duchess of Northumberland was particularly fond of this area, frequently taking her pony and trap to meet the home-coming Duke.

Cross the bridge and ascend right on the waymarked grassy trail, through dappled light in a glade of hairy birch and rowan, that gently ascends above the mile-high goal posts of Border Park Rugby Club to Jamie's Crags, then circles through a mix of light and shade, trees, flowers and tinkling burns to return to the banks of Kielder Burn. Follow the burn south on a needle-strewn path to the Duchess Brig. Note the many information plaques about the inhabitants of the forest.

Return south-west by the outward route, varying the final stretch by walking through the adventure play area before ascending to the Castle. If perhaps you don't feel like tackling the climbing frames, certainly have a go, and beat out a rhythm on the giant wooden xylophone.

WALK 3:
KIELDER VIADUCT & DEAD MAN CAIRN

Bakethin Car Park - Kielder Viaduct - Camp Rigg - Dead Man Cairn - Bakethin Reservoir - Border Counties Line - Bakethin Car Park.

Start/Finish: Bakethin Car Park (GR.631927), Information Board and picnic tables, ½ mile/0.8 km south of Kielder village by Butteryhaugh Bridge.

Type of walk: *A 2¾ mile/4.4 km walk of high interest and scenic delights, including the unique "Skew-Arched" Viaduct that carried the Border Counties railway over the North Tyne. The waymarked (orange arrowhead) route, on prepared paths, forest roads and grassy ways, with benches at the halfway mark, is never strenuous. Comfortable clothing and walking shoes will suffice for this Grade 1 walk of 1½/2 hours. Take the camera.*

Accommodation and refreshments: in/around Kielder village.

THE WALK: From Bakethin Car Park, leave by the prepared path ascending south to join the disused Border Counties line. *Born 1862, died 1958, this Tynedale life-line ran from Bellingham via Riccarton Junction to Newcastleton and Hawick.*

Turn left on to the tree-lined track leading to the lofty castellated deck of Kielder Viaduct. This unique viaduct – seven eye-catching spans with "Skew Arches", 392ft/119m long and rising 55ft/17m above the peat-stained North Tyne. At the southern end, descend left on a waymarked stepped path through the pleasing woods, (note the Information Board, above the east bank of the North Tyne) eventually to cross a tarmac road to a waymarked gate leading into the open pasture of Camp Rigg.

By a solitary pine lies the ¼ acre site of an Old English homestead with a banked earthwork and faint habitation marks.

The waymarked path enters the forest again, via a wicket gate, before ascending through bracken on to a forest track.

Turn right, i.e. south, with the waymark along the wide track, and just beyond the crest of the hill on the descending road an Information Board, in the conifers to the left, marks the mound of moss- and heather-covered stones of Dead Man Cairn.

Dead Man Cairn, a conspicuous circular pile thought to be 3,500/ 4,000 years old, sadly with evidence of robber holes, covers a Bronze Age burial cist, a shallow stone chamber covered by a single slab known as a cap-stone, in which the cadaver was placed in the foetal position. Alongside the body an urn containing possessions was

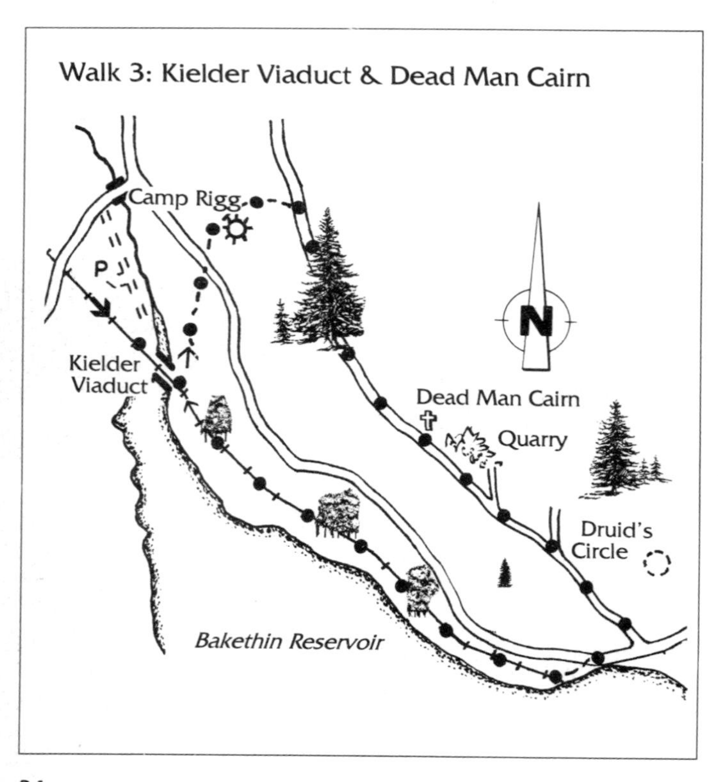

often placed, to assist the deceased into the next world.

Descend south-east with the forest track, past a large disused quarry on the left, forking right at the waymark, to reach a tarmac road above Bakethin Reservoir.

Cross the road and descend to the water's edge on a stepped and waymarked path, where fine views of the tranquil waters of Bakethin and its weir can be enjoyed. The way now utilises the disused rail track of the Border Counties, later to become the North British, Railway, for a delightful 1 mile/1.6 km stroll north through silver birch and alder to the Kielder viaduct. Judging by the variety of plant life beside the track and the volume of bird-song overhead, the wildlife also appreciates this pleasing habitat. A rocky mound at Bewshaugh, prior to the viaduct, carries a Viewpoint Information Board, pointing out items of interest on the skyline over Bakethin.

At the viaduct return with the outward route, to the picnic tables of Bakethin Car Park and journey's end.

Kielder viaduct

WALK 4: LEWIS BURN and AKENSHAW BURN

Lewisburn Picnic Place - Lewisburn Footbridge - Akenshaw Bridge - Forks Viewpoint - Lewisburn Bridge - Lewisburn Picnic Place.

Start/Finish: Lewisburn Car Park and Picnic Place (GR.636896). Signposted, ½ mile/0.8 km south-west from the C200 public road, 2½ miles/4 km south-south-east from Kielder village.

Type of walk: *2½ miles/4 km, with one small stepped ascent, alongside two of Kielder's finest burns, Lewis Burn and Akenshaw Burn. Travelling on waymarked forest paths, Bloody Bush Road and packhorse bridges, the walk is stimulating but never exhausting. This journey is a must for those who have an interest in all living things, or simply want to get away from it all. Trainers will suffice in dry conditions.*

Accommodation and refreshments: in/around Kielder village and Leaplish Waterside Park.

THE WALK: Leave Lewisburn Car Park and Picnic Place via the waymarked path east to the wooden footbridge crossing Lewis Burn. A delightful spot in a clearing by the burnside is equipped with picnic tables, washing/toilet facilities and maps highlighting walks, cycleways and bridleways. In summer, Lewis Burn is gently flowing, but as the scattering of large water-worn boulders indicate, it is not benign in winter, being subject to, as are many other Kielder burns, flash floods from the high fells.

Turn left, i.e. west and south-west, with the distinct waymarked path to follow Lewis Burn and later Akenshaw Burn until the pack-horse bridge is reached; a burnside path of character, through fine old conifers to the tune of hurrying water.

Alongside the burn small alder trees thrive, although they are overshadowed by established stands of Scots pine and Norway spruce, whose fine trunks carry nesting boxes for a variety of birds; a policy adopted in Kielder Forest since 1980 to avoid predation from foxes.

Admire the solid stone bridge over Akenshaw Burn, then turn left and cross to follow the forest road east for 250 yds/m to a waymarked wicket gate on the right.

The bridge and Bloody Bush toll road (now the forest road) were built around 1830 on the site of an old drove road across the Border Line. Coal from the mines of Lewisburn and Plashetts was transported by packhorse to Liddesdale and Hawick in Scotland. Lower down the dale, Falstone Coal Company took hard won coal from local mines as late as 1991, though not to send up Bloody Bush Road by packhorse!

A well-laid path winds and steps up the bluff to the conifers above, providing fine views of The Forks, the confluence of the two burns, and on the distant north-east skyline, the profile of Monkside and Berrymoor Edge.

Descend south between five glistening copper beech and the forest edge to the forest road below, and beyond, the stone arch of Lewisburn bridge.

Cross Lewis Burn and continue north-east on the forest road for ¾ mile/1.2 km, passing the houses at The Forks and a cluster of ponds on the left, to reach the car park of Lewisburn.

Natural though the ponds look, they were man-made many years ago. Today they support a rich variety of plants, insects and animal life, including spode newts, frogs, and toads, with the flowers of yellow flags, water avon, meadow sweet and bullrush surrounded by willow and alder.

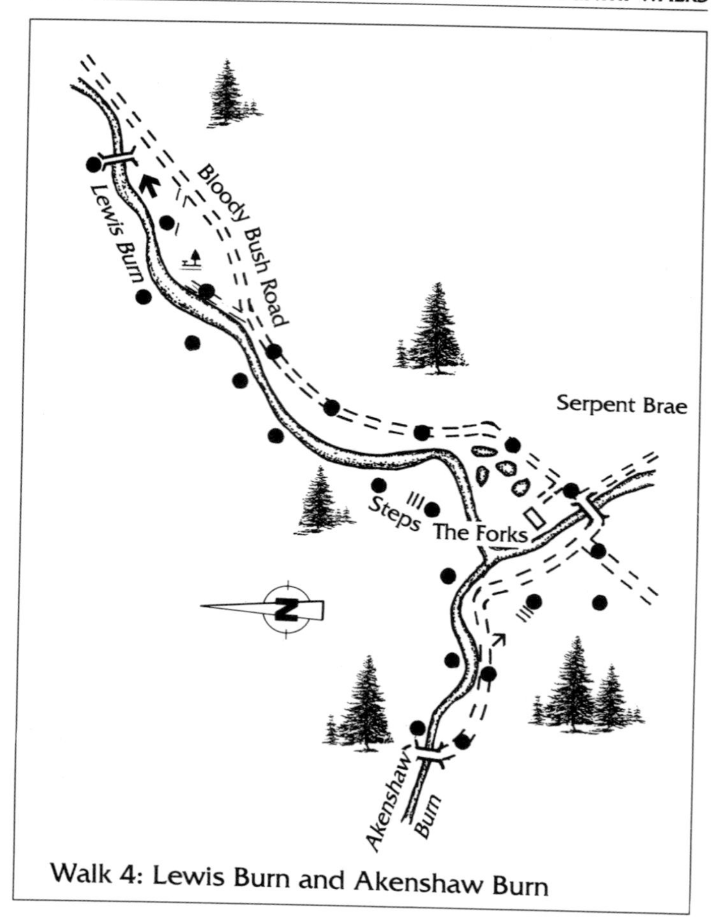

Walk 4: Lewis Burn and Akenshaw Burn

WALK 5:
BULL CRAG PENINSULA

Bull Crag Car Park - Otterstone - Old Tynedale Road - The Headland - Forest Ride - Bull Crag Car Park.

Start/Finish: Bull Crag Car Park and Picnic Place (GR.676864). Bull Crag is a dominant peninsula at the south end of Kielder Water, signposted via C200, 4 miles/ 6.4 km west of Kielder dam, 6½ miles/10.4 km south from Kielder village.

Type of walk: *This is a varied walk of 2 miles/3.2 km, where every corner turned presents new and pleasing views of Kielder Water and the conifer-clad hills. Forest roads, grassy paths, a scattering of seats and a section of the old North Tyne road allow easy walking on this Grade 1 route, a way rich in creatures of the forest and the water-side. Items of interest, with interpretive panels, blend with the panorama on this journey of 2 hours. Lightweight footwear and clothing is suitable, except in wet or winter conditions, when something more substantial is needed.*

Accommodation and refreshments: at Yarrow, Falstone, Leaplish and Tower Knowe.

THE WALK: Begin from the car park, picnic benches, information boards and toilets, overlooking the colourful anchorage of Whickhope and walk north with the forest road through an open stand of conifers. At a T-junction swing right, ascending north-east, still on a forest road. Ignore the track entering from the right and follow the waymarks north for ¼ mile/400m. Swing left into a small car parking area, then right between trees and wall, with the waymarks, before passing through a gate in the wall into a clearing leading to the water's edge.

Ahead is Jubilee Plantation, planted in 1977 to commemorate Queen Elizabeth's Silver Jubilee, close by Otterstone viewpoint. The Scots pines are especially outstanding against a backcloth of gentle water and folding fells.

Otterstone is an idyllic spot on a fine day, from its dolmen stone seats some of the finest views of Kielder can be savoured, from the prominent cone of Deadwater Fell 7½ miles/12 km to the north, in an arc east the tops of Greys Pike, Monkside and The Cross.

No doubt reluctantly, leave Otterstone along a thin waymarked path, descending east to the stile over the stone wall and into trees once more, via a cooling green tunnel. Emerge on to a forest road and swing left to the waterside and the tarmac remains of the old North Tyne Road. Turn right, i.e. east, with the road, until it sinks beneath the waters of Kielder at The Headland. This pre-Kielder Water road was the main highway through upper Tynedale, following the course of the North Tyne to Deadwater and on across the Border into Scotland; little remains visible today. From The Headland, Kielder dam with its prominent valve tower can be seen, a mere 1¼ miles/ 2 km east over the water, by foot a laboured 6½ miles/10.4 km.

Waymarks, an orange arrowhead or an Otter footprint, lead to a forest road heading south-west from The Headland. For the purist, follow the road south-west until it plunges into the trees before striking south along a ride to the south shore. A path travels west with the tree-lined shoreline to the starting car park.

For those wishing to extend this pleasurable walk, leave the forest road at an inlet and follow the Otter footprint waymarks, for a short sample of the Kielder Water Challenge Circuit (KWCC) Marathon Walk as it hugs the shoreline, to the car park with its picnic tables.

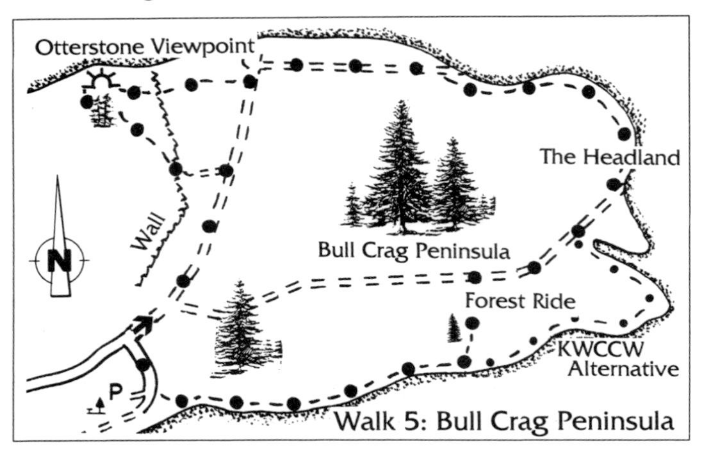

Walk 5: Bull Crag Peninsula

WALK 6:

THE BELLING and THE DAM

Hawkhope Car Park - Gordon's Walls - Belling Causeway - The Belling - Belling Crag - Falstone Drift - Hawkhope.

Start/Finish: Hawkhope Car Park (GR.707882), at the north end of Kielder dam. 1 mile/1.6 km west of Falstone and 1 mile/1.6 km north, via the dam road, from the C200.

Type of walk: *This delightful waterside walk, regarded by many as Kielder Water's finest, of 2 miles/3.2 km can be extended by a stroll across the dam and a visit to the commemorative stones nearby. The route winds by the water-lapped north shore of the reservoir to the causeway and sylvan delights of The Belling peninsula. The waymarked trail, orange arrowhead and Otter footprint, is via forest roads and woodland paths for this Grade 1 walk, with informative panels discreetly positioned. Rich in history, flora, fauna and fine views, the walk takes no more than 1½ hours, requiring only sound trainers or light-weight boots as footwear.*

Accommodation and refreshments: at Falstone, Stannersburn and Yarrow.

THE WALK: Leave Hawkhope Car Park, picnic benches and toilets, with the waymarks at its north-east corner, to join the North Haul Road, a major forestry access road running the entire 10 miles/16 km of the north shore of Kielder Water. Swing left, i.e. west-north-west, with the wide road for 200 yds/m to a waymarked trail, leading left through well-spaced conifers. For the next ¾ mile/1.2 km the way winds on a needle-strewn and root-scattered path, surrounded by waterside sights and sounds and enhanced by the fragrances of the forest.

Note the Information Board at Gordon's Walls, explaining the history of the overgrown 19th century farmstead, thought to have

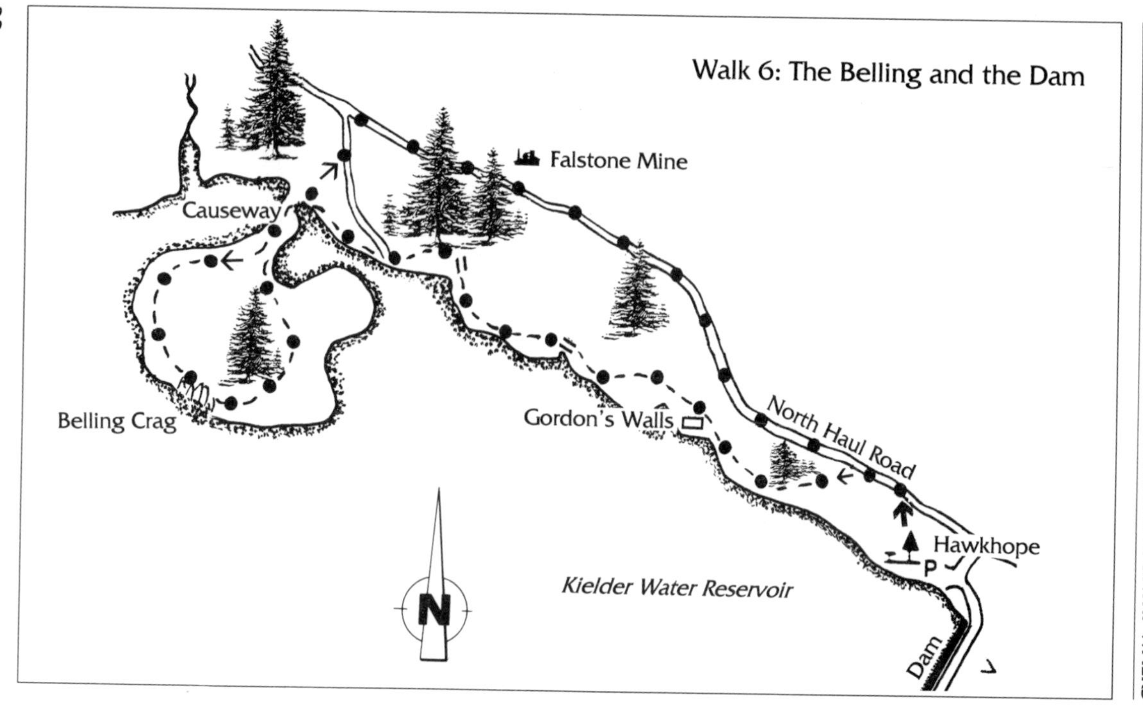
Walk 6: The Belling and the Dam
Falstone Mine
Causeway
Belling Crag
Gordon's Walls
North Haul Road
Hawkhope
P
Kielder Water Reservoir
Dam

stood on the site of an ancient bastle - a defensive farm house built some 200ft/60m above the then valley floor, Tynedale being much favoured by marauding Border reivers.

When The Belling, cloaked and green, hoves into view, the marked trail crosses a forest road as it approaches the narrow causeway.

Once across, the trail splits. Take the right fork encircling The Belling anticlockwise as the path, resounding with bird song, rises and falls to reach Belling Crag.

The Crag is a long-since abandoned quarry cliff-face of Scremerston sandstone, its lower reaches now submerged, that provides dramatic views of the south shore of Kielder Water, the valve tower and the dam. An Information Board pinpoints the views, but do take care on the cliff top.

Leave the shoreline, ascending the sun-dappled path, through the central conifers returning to the causeway. Now is decision time. A circular return on forest roads including nearly 1 mile/1.6 km on the Long Haul Road, much used by timber lorries and mountain bikes; along which the only item of interest is the disused Falstone Drift Mine, born 1895, worked off and on for 96 years, finally dying in 1991 - the last coal mine in Tynedale. Or a return on the bewitching trail of our outward journey, with a fresh set of views: the choice is yours.

The stones, commemorating the opening of Kielder Water, and the dam path lie south-east and south from Hawkhope and provide an interesting and scenically pleasing extension to the Belling walk.

CHAPTER 2

ADVENTUROUS RAMBLES: With the Curlew's Cry

Seven walks for the adventurous and the naturally curious, revealing yet more of Kielder and Tynedale; walks to take the walker just that little bit further. In addition to many items of interest along the way, each walk has a highlight or outstanding feature only seen or appreciated by actually completing the walk. The walks, that embrace the banks of the North Tyne and its spectacular burns, provide seldom seen sights and sounds of Tynedale's forests, reservoirs, moors and crags while treading the ways of the reiver, the cadger and the preacher man, allowing the adventurer and the curious an additional taste of Kielder denied to many visitors. The walks are longer, though no less pleasing, than in Chapter 1; not all are waymarked or noted on the OS maps. Navigation should not however be a problem if this guide is taken on the journey.

The routes cover forest roads and paths, burnside ways and moorland tracks, and even on the open fell where only thin sheep traces are followed the walker can confidently rely on a keen eye, a sure step and the guide to make the journey a pleasure. There are more and higher ascents than in Chapter 1, but at no point are they arduous for the average walker, indeed, fit and young enthusiasts will probably not notice, or admit to, any appreciable change of angle.

Walking equipment should be governed by weather conditions, both actual and potential, but, since conditions underfoot vary from mile to mile, season to season, it is advisable always to wear walking boots/shoes. The walks offer numerous diverse views of forest, fell and watercourse, plus opportunities to observe first hand the shy and not so shy inhabitants of this intriguing heart of Britain; a camera and binoculars are recommended.

All routes are circular or lollipop walks (i.e. the same short section will be used for the walk-out and the walk-in); and all have parking facilities at, or close to, the start. Should the appetite be whetted for a longer challenge, several of the walks in Chapter 2 include small sections of the longer, higher walks detailed in Chapter 3.

JUST THAT LITTLE BIT FURTHER
- At a Glance

Leap off to Smales in Walk 7 and find, if you can, the delightful gorge-in-miniature of Smales Burn. Walk 8 provides a balanced mix of airy fell, rock and tree-lined dene and a winding way with the North Tyne river; whereas Walk 9 tramps the banks of the at times savage, but always picturesque, Lewis Burn on a packhorse path. Walk 10 tracks by burn and open fell to an ancient castle and hawker's ford; in contrast to the sylvan delights of Sidwood and the bastles by Tarset Burn, in Walk 11. Walk 12 seeks out preacher Sandy Peden's sandstone cloister on Ravenshill Moor, and finally Walk 13 climbs to the grandstand of Cat Cairn with surprise views to the south.

Walk 7: Smale's Leap and the Smuggler's Way

WALK 7: SMALE'S LEAP and THE SMUGGLER'S WAY

Stannersburn - White Side Rigg - Smales Burn - Smale's Leap - Alternative Pennine Way - Stannersburn.

Start/Finish: Stannersburn (GR.722867) 1 mile/1.6 km east of Kielder Water dam. Parking in the village; take care not to obstruct access.

Type of walk: *A circular walk of 3½ miles/5.6 km on forest roads, waymarked grassy paths and sections of faint narrow sheep tracks. After a quiet start the route soon assumes the mantle of an uncharted expedition, as the green gorge of Smale's or Smuggler's Leap is eventually discovered, with the walk-out offering extensive views of Tynedale. Walking boots are needed for the wet sections and ophidiaphobes need caution as adders favour the warm stones by Smales Burn. Take this guide and your sense of direction.*

Accommodation and refreshments: in Stannersburn and nearby Falstone.

THE WALK: South of the scattered houses of Stannersburn a waymarked ("APW" - Alternative Pennine Way) gate below a radio mast leads on to a forest road that snakes southwards over the open fell for ½ mile/0.8 km to cross White Side Rigg. Here the conifers are met, but only to frame the views, never to smother them, as the road winds south in descent. Ignore two roads entering from the right on the zigzag and at the crossroads take the sharp left, i.e. east, to the flat land by Smales Burn.

A forestry quarry can be seen ahead, as can a flat bridge across Smales Burn. These quarries provided sandstone for forest roads, for it was around Smales that the first conifers were planted by the

Forestry Commission in 1926. Do not cross the burn but turn right, i.e. south, on to a faint burnside track. Follow this as it runs parallel with the burn for several hundred yards until the waterway appears to vanish into a tree-clad miniaturised gorge.

So narrow is this gorge there are parts where the sides appear almost to touch, an ideal hiding place for contraband. Indeed, this very spot lay on the North Tyne smuggling route, being known as Smuggler's or Smale's Leap. Care is also needed should you be tempted to enter the gorge, for the way is slippery and in places the rock unstable. A cautious exploration into the dusky light of this moss-covered, fern-clad glen of spirits brings high rewards.

Return to the bridge and cross the forest road to a rocky outcrop by Smales Burn. Ascend this fine vantage point and enjoy the sights and sounds of the forest fringe.

A faint path is visible in the grass below; walk north between the encroaching conifers to a waymarked (APW) gate on to the open fell. Ahead a flat rush-ridden pasture rises north to meet a grassy cart track beyond a solitary stone post on White Side Rigg. Ascend the cart track to a waymarked gate on to the outward forest road; descend northwards to Stannersburn.

To the north and east lies upper Tynedale, a valley of ancient woodland and winding rivers, where Thorneyburn Common rises above Donkley Wood and Stokoe High Crags top Birks Moor.

In Stannersburn stands The Pheasant Inn, previously called The Crown, a pub much favoured by the miners of Plashetts. After the colliery had mined its last tub of coal, the miners, in appreciation, left their lamps to hang forever in the bar.

By the pub car park stands a simple cross, dedicated, by their comrades, to Luftwaffe air crew who perished on these lonely hills.

WALK 8:
SLATY FORD: THE DROVER'S WAY

Falstone - Slaty Ford - Old Hall - North Tyne - Donkleywood - Falstone.

Start/Finish: Falstone (GR.724875) 1 mile/1.6 km east from the mighty dam of Kielder Water and ½ mile/0.8 km north of the Kielder to Bellingham Road.

Type of walk: *A varied walk of 7 miles/11.2 km, by windswept drove and sheltered haugh, offering the walker a fine panorama of Upper Tynedale, in addition to an insight into its diverse wildlife. Never severe, the trail covers country lanes, cart tracks, grassy bridleways and pastured river banks. Gentle ascents total 515ft/157m on this scenic, non huff and puff, journey through time and space. Graded 2, it is advisable to wear walking shoes/boots and outdoor clothing for this 3½/4 hour walk.*

Refreshments: Inn and cafe at Falstone.

THE WALK: Leave the village of Falstone from the Blackcock Inn, walking north under the ageing North British Rail bridge to turn right on to the country lane, south-east and east for 1¼ miles/2 km, passing en route the now defunct Falstone station.

The Border Counties railway, later to become the North British Railway, opened Falstone in 1862; extending the platform, the coal siding and the buildings in 1895.

Ascend east with the lane, past the owl-guarded Rectory, to a strip of majestic Scots pine at a waymarked and signposted junction - "Unsuitable for Motor Vehicles". Turn left on to the farm road, i.e. north and north-north-east by the old stone gate posts, as the gated way maintains a straight line for ¾ mile/1.2 km to the entrance of Ryeclose Farm.

The drystone walls of northern Northumberland are constructed on the double wall principle, with two walls leaning in towards each other, the centre packed with fillers or "chatter". Keep an eye out for a "smoot" along the way, small openings in the wall allowing sheep but not cattle to pass through. To the left, above the bare sandstone of Kingsley Crag, stands a "currick", an old stone sheep/shepherd's shelter.

Continue north-north-east with the rutted, gated cart track for a further ¾ mile/1.2 km over open country. Note the track ahead disappearing over the skyline, a local drove road of yesteryear, leading down Tynedale to Bellingham mart. Above, to the north, the Sitka of Falstone Forest stands guard as the water-worn slabs of Slaty Ford are reached through yet another gate.

Thorney Burn, a gentle burn in summer, washes over the sandstone before hurrying down the overgrown steps and stairs of Hillhouse Clints dene.

After admiring the ford return through the gate to a stile in the wall leading into grassy moorland; follow the waymarks south-west and south-south-east descending with the burn. Continue with the path, through the wicket gates via Hill House, to pass two isolated stone gateposts before joining a disused rail track.

Tynedale's lifeline, the Counties Line, ran from Bellingham to Riccarton junction, carting coal and countryfolk.

More gates and one field lead to a tarmac road by Old Hall Cottage; turn right, i.e. west, with the road for 600yds/m to the signpost ("Donkleywood") on the left.

Descend to the footbridge over Ryeclose Burn leading to a stiled pasture with a waymarked path, (access and waymarks arranged by Northumberland National Park) to another stile by a solitary oak. With a guiding fence on the right, further gates and stiles lead to Camp Cottage and its ruined bastle. From the cottage walk west-south-west, crossing several stiles and swinging right into the riverside wood. Walk west through the oak and alder, where the sounds of the river are music to the ear, and watch out for the sparrowhawks who find these woods a happy hunting ground, leaving via the stone dyke on the right. Pass through a hole in the wall to follow the waymarks half right, i.e. north-west, over coarse pasture to the bridge, railbed and cottages of Low Donkleywood.

Once across the line it is but a short step north to modern Donkleywood.

In 1166 the Bellinghams of Bellingham, foresters to William, King of Scotland, had a hunting lodge at Donkleywood, which grew in the 13th century to be one of the seven most important settlements in Tynedale.

Leave by swinging left past the village green ascending with the road to the strip of Scots pine encountered on the outward journey. From the T-junction descend west and north-west for a scenic return to the smoking lumbs of Falstone.

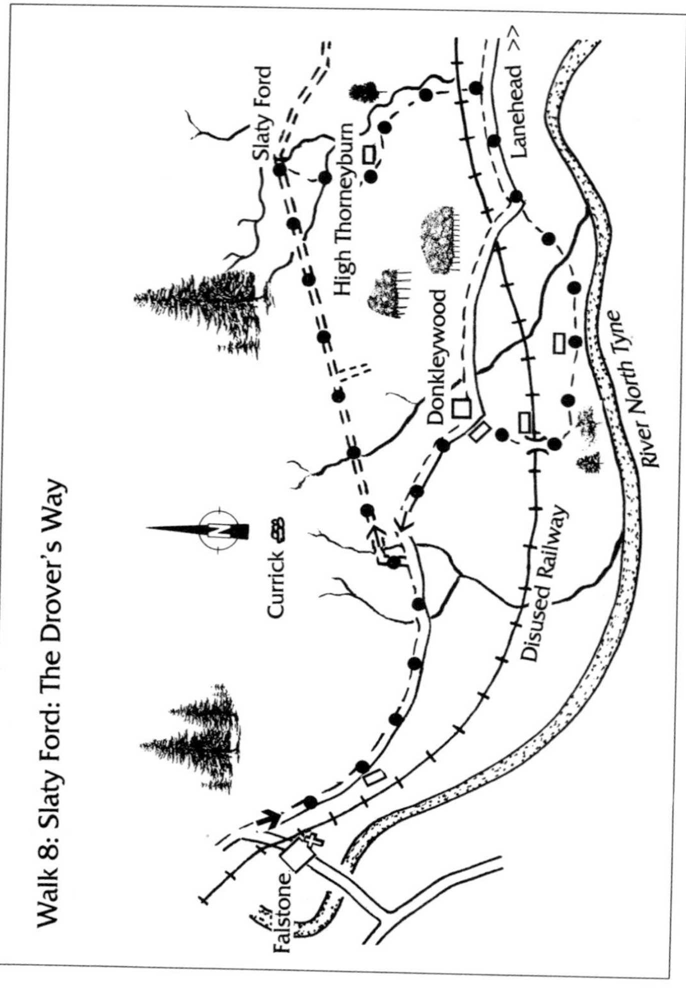

WALK 9:
BY LEWIS BURN TO HIGH LONG HOUSE

Lewisburn Car Park & Picnic Place - The Forks - Lewis Burn - Low Long House - High Long House - Peat Sike - Lewisburn Car Park.

Start/Finish: Lewisburn Car Park & Picnic Place (GR.636896) signposted from the C200 public road, 3 miles/4.8 km south-south-east from Kielder village.

Type of walk: *A beautiful burn of changing moods, rich in wildlife, history and scenic beauty is Lewis Burn, our guide for 4¼ miles/6.8 km of this 6½ mile/10.4 km walk. William Eure, writing to Cardinal Wolsey in 1536, observed: "the rebels of Tynedale abydings is in a place called Lushburn Howles (Lewisburn)." A journey of serene solitude, Graded 2 in summer, 4 when the burn is in spate, with gradual ascents totalling 550ft/168m. The partially waymarked route by forest roads and grassy path (with 1½ miles/2.4 km of wild walking along the burnside or burn bed) presents no navigational problems. Allow 3½/4 hours, walking shoes/boots are recommended.*

Accommodation and refreshments: at Falstone and Kielder.

THE WALK: From Lewisburn Picnic Place walk west, via the Exit sign, to the forest road junction, turning right for a delightful ½ mile/ 0.8 km to The Forks. The ponds on the right, man-made but now mature, are havens for aquatic life.

One of The Forks cottages is probably 17th century and was previously a social history museum.

Prior to Lewisburn bridge, swing left, i.e. south-south-east, on to a dirt and grass track by the east bank of Lewis Burn; our companion for the next 3 miles/4.8 km.

Head south-south-west, and as the valley narrows the stands of spruce keep a respectful distance from the burn, allowing a profusion of deciduous trees and ground cover to flourish. The colours on nature's palette are best appreciated in autumn, when the valley is aflame with yellows, rusts and reds, where even the shy grey heron stands out against the benign waters of the burn. Every corner turned reveals a new and exciting prospect; first, seams of exposed strata, folds of sandstone interbedded with successions of coal, shales and limestones, known as The Scremerston Coals.

As the burn is crossed via a functional, featureless bridge, there stands on the right a stone packhorse bridge, one of many built in 1828 to ease the transportation, by pack pony, of the 4,000 tons of coal produced annually from the Lewisburn drift mines (see Walk 17). Beyond, a walled pasture contains a long-abandoned shieling heralding the remains of Low Long House, almost hidden in the tall grass on a raised mound.

When peace returned to Tynedale in the 18th century, the defensive bastles were abandoned and farmers built a Long House nearby. The house and byre were under the one roof, both entered by the same door leading on to a cross passage behind the kitchen fire. Two such farms stood by Lewis Burn, Low Long House and High Long House. Low is now demolished, High is still occupied.

To the right a ride with a grassy track ascends west; ahead the track narrows through the trees.

[NOTE: For those who do not wish to tackle the burnside scramble to High Long House, or should Lewis Burn be in spate preventing safe passage, the ride allows an easy return to Lewisburn car park.]

At the crumbling walled enclosure, follow the thin path through the trees on to the grassy west bank, narrowed by encroaching conifers and forcing passage on to the burn bed. Ahead, overshadowed by towering larch, an elbow in the burn is jammed with immense sandstone boulders and it is here that care is needed, 1) to identify the faint path, 2) to negotiate safe passage. THIS POINT INDICATES TO ALL WALKERS, FORWARD, OR BACK TO LOW LONG HOUSE AND THE RIDE.

This boulder-strewn ribbon of delight continues to guide us past the silent reminders of long-gone shepherds and their shielings, and miners and their mines. Now the solitude is so intense it can almost be heard above the tumbling linn as it pours its peat-stained waters into a bottomless bible black pool. As the burn continues south-west another angled bend below an overhang necessitates a burn crossing. Once the bend is passed, re-cross to the west bank prior to the junction of Lishaw Burn and Lewis Burn, from where our guide leads us west, via its north bank, to the now visible High Long House by a forest road.

The prefix "High" may have originally been given because this Long House was higher up the burn, or simply because the house acquired a second storey.

Beyond High Long House, turn right by the bridge, i.e. north, ascending with the road for the 3 miles/4.8 km return, a journey of contrast and easy passage. After approximately 1 mile/1.6 km, between Forking Sike and Peat Sike, a forest road enters from the left and the now wide ride toils up right from Low Long House.

On the western skyline stands Caplestone Fell with Elliot's Pike and a scattering of cairns, reputed to be route markers used by the Liddesdale reiving family of Elliot returning to their peles of Park and Larriston.

As incoming roads from the left and Peat Sike are put behind us the way veers right, i.e. north-east, offering fine views of Oh Me Edge, Blakehope Nick (on the Forest Drive) and Berrymoor Edge, before descending to the packhorse bridge at The Forks. Cross over Lewis Burn and bear left with the main forest road returning north and north-east for a well-deserved picnic at Lewisburn Car Park.

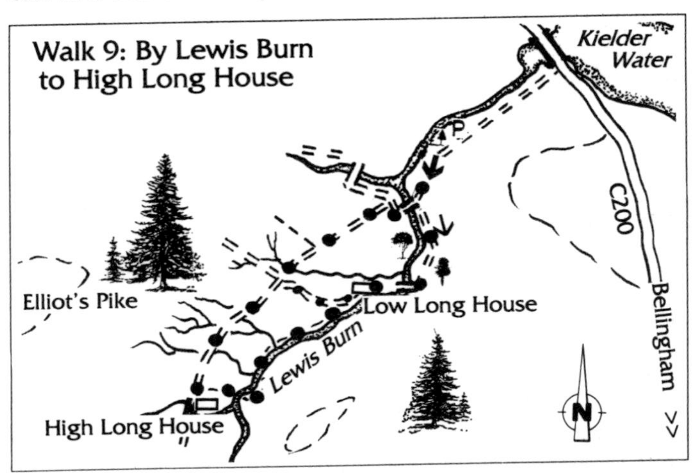

WALK 10:
DALLY CASTLE & CADGER FORD (TRADE AND TRAGEDY)

Chirdon Burn Bridge- Birks - Dally Castle - Cadger Ford - Whitchester - Snabdaugh Moor - Chirdon Burn Bridge.

Start/Finish: Layby/car park at the south-east end of Chirdon Burn Bridge (GR.783849). On the unclassified road running south of the river North Tyne, 1½ miles/2.4 km south of Lanehead and 5 miles/8 km west of Bellingham.

Type of walk: *By the tree-lined murmurings of Chirdon Burn to the stones of yesterday's castle, then on to cross Cadger Ford and explore the crag-strewn fells, where curlews cry. For the entire 4½ miles/7.2 km this walk experiences the riot of isolation that is Tynedale. Public bridleways, waymarked by Northumberland National Park, take the walker along narrow lanes, cart tracks and grassy paths; solid trainers suffice in dry conditions; when wet, boots are recommended. Graded 2, this is a walk to potter around, taking 2½/3 hours.*

Accommodation and refreshments: in/around Bellingham.

THE WALK: Cross the narrow, high arched bridge of Chirdon Burn, whose solid stones were put in place in 1821, then immediately turn left to Birks. The lane ascends west and south-west, passing Birks Cottages and circling Birks before rejoining Chirdon Burn, winding reflectively by, for a pleasing stretch in the company of silver birch, ash and beech to the House, Mill and Castle of Dally.

An early pele tower, Dally Castle was built on the spur of a glacial ridge by a Scot, David Lindsay, around 1237 (Tynedale was at the time in Scotland). Never completely finished, this small tower (outer walls 25 yds x 18 yds) remained as a stronghold until the Union of the

Crowns in 1603, from whence its "decaie" began. Now a crumbled ruin, many of its stones reside in the walls of the mill, the house and surrounding stane dykes.

The lane continues west and south-west for nearly ½ mile/0.8 km before the ranks of Sitka are met. Here, glance over Chirdon Burn on to Snabdaugh Moor and Miller Hill where mounds and grooves indicate the coal miner's hand and the packhorse's hoof.

For the mile (1.6 km) south-west to Cadger Ford the way is lined with conifers, mature trees allowing shafts of sun to illuminate the forest floor, with copper beech, cherry, chestnut, cypress, larch and ash adorning the avenue. Chirdon farmhouse and bridge eventually come into view backed by Gallow Hill. Turn left at the signpost (Public Bridleway "Watson's Walls 2 miles"), taking care to close the gate before crossing the burn on one of two bridges, between which lies Cadger Ford.

Still visible, marked by two lines of stones, Cadger Ford has served soldier, drover, cleric and cadger (hawker or country carrier) through the centuries.

A wide stony cart track gently ascends east past Chirdon Farm (records detail an old water-powered flour mill at Chirdon), on to Chirdon Moor, with the cairn-capped Whitchester Crags prominent to the right, weather-worn exposed beds of sandstone lying within the base rock known as Scremerston Coals. After ½ mile/0.8 km, at an angle in the farm road, the views north and east, of the Border Line and Tarset valley, explode into view. Go left with the grassy track, descending to a burnside gate bearing a blue arrowhead marked "Public Bridleway", a way that steadily rises through bracken, to the wall leading east to Whitchester Farm.

Mentioned as an agricultural holding in the 15th century, today's Georgian farmhouse is typical of many in the area, a symmetrical, solid, low-pitched building.

At the north side of the farm a waymarked post directs the walker left, i.e. north, across the green expanse of Snabdaugh Moor (pronounced Snabduf). Keep initially right then swing left on to a twin track to the next posted waymark, thereafter the route undulates over the sloping shoulders of the moor, with the white walls of Bent House on the valley floor providing a fine marker. Above Chirdon Burn and Dally Castle beyond, the path swings right, i.e. north-east, the grass-covered grooves underfoot suggesting packhorse trails, and the mounds below Hart Crags, redundant mines. Descend to two waymarked gates leading to a verdant haugh. On the far side of this pasture stands a solitary gnarled ash marking the exit gate; stroll left to the lane for the final yards to Chirdon Burn Bridge.

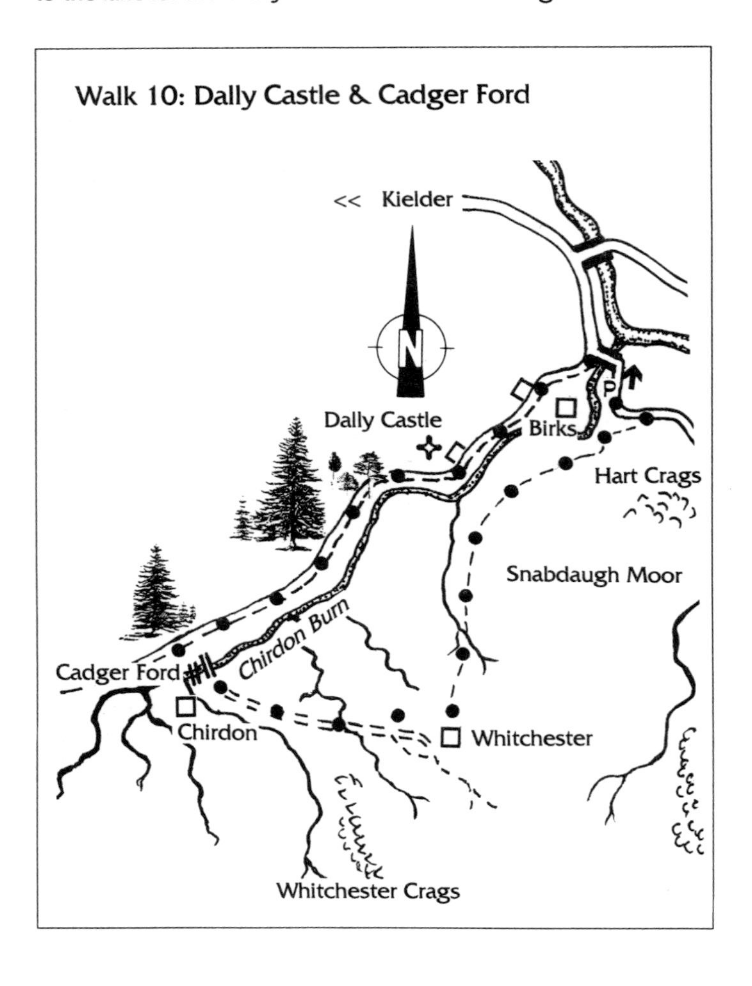

WALK 11:

SIDWOOD: THE REIVER'S TRAIL

Sidwood Picnic Place - Tarset Burn - Woodhouse - Waterhead - Shilla Hill - Barty's Pele Bog Head - Black Middens - Sidwood Picnic Place.

Start/Finish: Sidwood Picnic Place and Car Park (GR.776892). 2 miles/3.2 km north-west from Greenhaugh village by signposted lane. 3½ miles/5.5 kms of picturesque walking in the valley of Tarset.

Type of walk: *A pleasing circular route of high interest by waymarked forest roads and paths, pasture fields and country lanes, its length peppered with the "caste-doune" stones of ruined bastles, grim reminders of not so long ago, when the Liddesdale fighting families of Armstrong, Elliot and Croser, intent on plunder, poured over the Border. Graded 2, with no appreciable ascents, the walk requires stout footwear and 2-2½ hours of your time. A sylvan delight in spring and autumn colours, brimful with wildlife where every stone has a tale to tell.*

Accommodation and refreshments: at Greenhaugh (refreshments only) and Bellingham.

THE WALK: Sidwood Picnic Place, so idyllic it is hard to leave, is forsaken by the forest road running north-west past whitewashed Sidwood Cottage; where a Reiver's Way waymark guides us right on to a wooded path descending to the silver birch banks of Tarset Burn. Swing left with the elbow of the burn, as the rustic, gated path winds between burn and pasture field to a footbridge. This bridge is for our return journey, so, for the moment, continue ahead, i.e. north-west on the waymarked path by the burn.

Such was the reputation of the area surrounding upper Tynedale for lawlessness, it prompted the Merchant Adventurers' Company of Newcastle in 1554 to issue a decree that "no free brother of this Fellowship shall take non apprentice to serve in the Fellowship of non such as is or shall be born or brought up in Tynedale, Redesdale or any siclike places in pain of £20."

Surrounded by eye-catching forest, fell and tinkling burn it is easy to miss the grass-grown mound on the left bearing the scattered stones of Woodhouse (Hill-house) Bastle.

Bastles, dating from 1520-1640, were fortified farmhouses with solid walls 4½ feet thick, a ceiling supported by rough-hewn oak or ash, and a roof of thatch or stone slabs pinned with sheep bones. One small door and narrow windows preventing easy entry.

Less than ½ mile/0.8 km ahead, beyond the pasture, stands the cottage of Waterhead where the massive cornerstones of Waterhead Bastle now reside in the nearby stone dyke.

Waterhead dates back to the mid-16th century and was occupied until the mid-19th century. Jenkin Hunter, an occupant of Waterhead, registered a strong complaint against the reiving Armstrongs, "who in warlyk maner ran an open daytime foray to Black Middens, Hillhouse, Waterhead, Starr Head, Bog Head and Highfield, raysing fire and driving many nolt, sheep and goats away."

Blacklinn Burn, beyond the cottage, is crossed by ford or footbridge on to a waymarked forest road ascending left; as the road levels out a waymarked grass path swings right into a re-planted stand of spruce. The winding way to Shilla Hill (Starr Head) Bastle is topped with grey and "decaied" stone out of which a rowan grows.

Starr Head, due to its elevated position, acted as a lookout for its immediate neighbours when visitors from the north threatened.

Descend north, with the distinct path, into the established spruce leading to the beech and birch banks of Tarset Burn; winding north-west for ¾ mile/1.2 km to discover Barty (Bartholomew) Milburn's Pele at Bog Head.

Known also as Corbie's Castle, the pele was raided in the late 1600s by Scots reivers who made off with Barty's sheep. Barty and neighbour Corbett Jack of Starr Head set off in pursuit; unable to trace his stock Barty replaced them with a Scots herd. Unfortunately, they were seen and chased to Redesdale Head and in the ensuing tussle Corbett Jack died and the two Scots were slain, one by decapitation. Barty, though wounded, carried Jack's body back to Bog Head: said the Bereaved of the Beheaded, "His heid spang alang the heather like an onion."

The nearby crumbling Long House, fringing the ill-drained haugh, was built, as with many others in the 18th century, as peace slowly

Springtime in Sidwood

Along the Belling Peninsula

Ridge End Burn

Kielder Water sunset

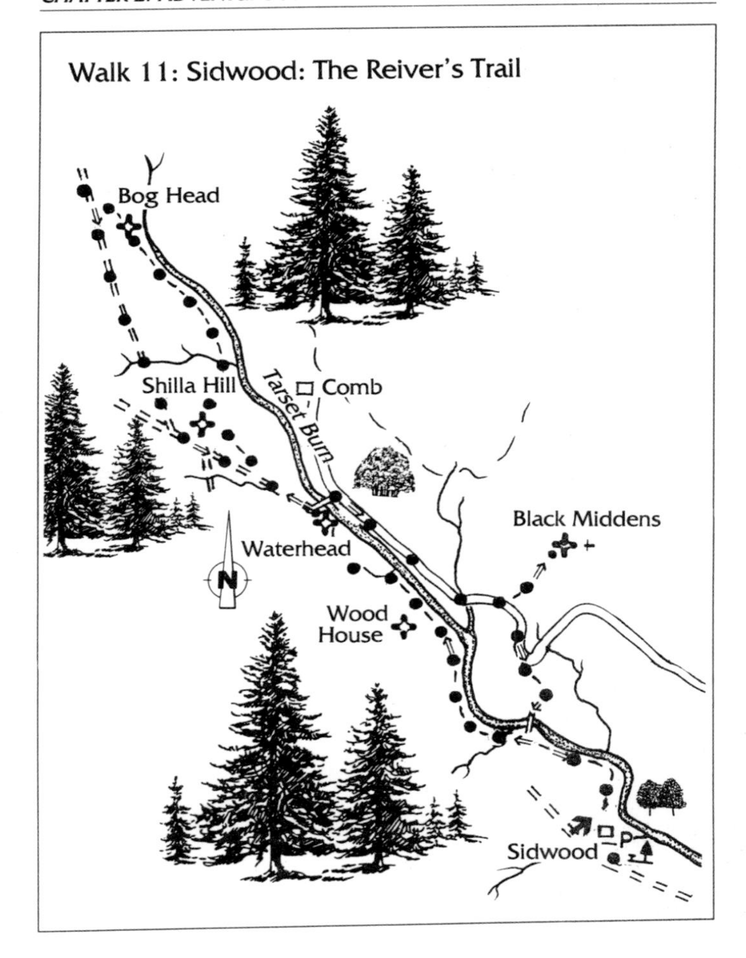
Walk 11: Sidwood: The Reiver's Trail
Bog Head
Shilla Hill
Tarset Burn
Comb
Waterhead
Black Middens
N
Wood
House
P
Sidwood

returned. The house and byre are under one roof, both being entered by the same door.

Pass north by Bog Head to the waymarked forest road; descend left taking two left forks en route to Waterhead, then cross Tarset Burn swinging right along a waymarked road. Beyond, a choice of crossings is offered at Black Burn, prior to Black Middens car park, by footbridge, road bridge or ford, an indicator of the frequency of flash-floods. Turn left, i.e. north, at the waymarked swing gate rising to Black Middens Bastle.

This partially restored stronghold and nearby 18th century cottage provide a clear picture of past life and death in Tarset valley.

Return to the car park and walk east with the road to the U-turn where waymarks guide our party south through pastures green to the banks of Tarset Burn, crossed by a wooden footbridge; go left at the rustic wicket gate on to the outward path from Sidwood. This burnside tree-lined way, with West Wood flourishing on the opposite bank, provides a fitting finale as it winds through colourful rhododendron for a thoroughly deserved picnic.

Kielder Castle

WALK 12:

FROM CASTLE TO CAVE

Kielder Castle - Ravenshill - Ravenshill Moor - Peden's Cave - Chubbies Knowe - Kielder Castle.

Start/Finish: Kielder Castle Visitor Centre (GR.633935), above the village of Kielder. Parking at Castle Wood.

Type of walk: *A circular walk of 5½ miles/8.8 km, with a height gain of 656ft/200m. Graded 2, the journey needs no more than 3 hours, over forest roads, thin moorland paths and along the railbed of the disused Border Counties line. A walk that is alive with the creatures of the forest and fell, steeped in fact and legend of yesteryear and revealing a galaxy of unexpected views. Walking boots advised.*

Accommodation and refreshments: including a well-equipped caravan and camp site, in and around Kielder village.

THE WALK: From Kielder Castle Visitor Centre, walk beyond the traffic roundabout, with the public toilets on the right, on to a forest road travelling north-west.

Built in 1775 as a shooting lodge for the Duke of Northumberland, Kielder Castle is now an imposing visitor centre featuring free information and exhibitions including the "Birds of Kielder" Experience, opened in 1993 by the Prince of Wales. The Longpack shop stocks an extensive range of gifts, guidebooks and pamphlets, plus a range of outdoor clothing and equipment; a cafe and restaurant provide welcome refreshments.

Take the first footpath on the right through the trees, a mix of species alive with birdsong and forest dwellers, to ascend on to a forest road running north-west. Turn left to pass above Ravenshill Farm, reaching a rough track on the right along which we travel north for ½ mile/0.8 km, through a recently-harvested spruce stand, to a stile over the fence at GR.628952.

Ahead the fells open up over Ravenshill Moor, with a rash of sandstone crags (our destination) on the skyline above Lightpipe

Sike, a fitting backcloth for the curlew's cry. The way progresses north on narrow sheep tracks, over heather and tussock grass above Lightpipe Sike and an ailing sheep stell, to the centre of the crags, where a wind-bent tree appears to grow out from the weathered sandstone. A few yards west is the small shelter of Peden's Cave (GR.628957).

Sandy Peden, a Hawick covenanter of the mid-17th century, who, because of having signed and adhered to the Scottish National Covenant of 1638, was forced to preach from secluded pulpits. The black mass of Rubers Law above Denholm has a summit outcrop known as Peden's Pulpit. Driven from Scotland by the episcopal hand of Claverhouse's dragoons after 1660 (The Killing Times), Peden held prayer meetings in North Tynedale, e.g. Padon Hill, and is reputed to have lived in the cave. Sir Walter Scott saw the other side of the covenanters, "hard and dour men who - Prove their doctrine orthodox, By apostolic blows and knocks."

Leave the cave by ascending, beyond an electric pole, to the fence guiding us north to the twin gates at GR.628959. Turn left on to the rough Deadwater Fell road, descending south-west into the forest in a series of extended zigzags. First west, then left, i.e. south-east, at the junction the next corner swings right, i.e. west-south-west, to a second junction; turn left, i.e. south, to the open pastures of Lightpipe and the road to Kielder.

The views to the south, over the chimney pots of Kielder, are of Bakethin, whose dam/weir was built to ensure that no matter what volume of water is drawn from Kielder Water the upper reaches would always remain submerged and not reveal unsightly mud flats. Bakethin Reservoir and the surrounding forest fringes are designated as a nature conservation area.

Cross the road, walk right for approximately 75yds/m to a layby to mount the opposite grass and tree-lined verge on to the railbed of the now redundant Border Counties/North British Railway line. Turn left, i.e. south-south-east, for a brisk and pleasing walk on the old track for 1 mile/1.6 km to Kielder village.

The line, opened in July 1862, linked Bellingham to Riccarton Junction and thence to the Scottish Borders, providing a lifeline for the folk of Tynedale and an economic means of transporting coal for the coal companies. Everything and everyone travelled the line, be it household supplies on the up-train, or old Geordie on his last journey on the down-train. All ended in 1958.

Continue to the fork, taking the right leg through the old sawmill to Kielder village via Castle Drive.

Designed by Thomas Sharp, each forest village was planned to have its own church, inn, shops and school.

Beyond, a winding road crosses the bridge and ascends to the Castle Visitor Centre.

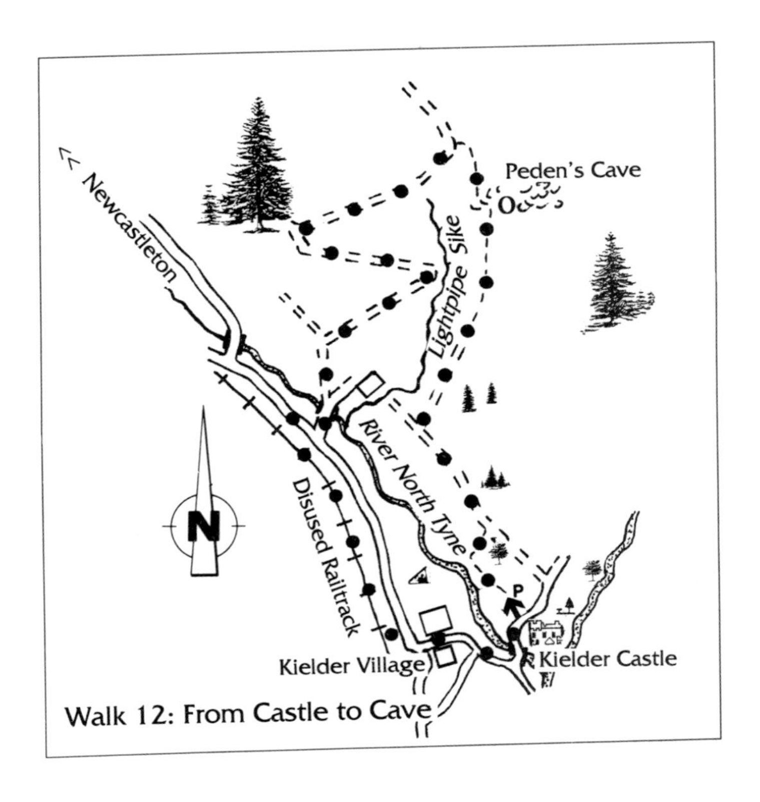

Walk 12: From Castle to Cave

WALK 13:
CAT CAIRN & PURDON PIKE

Butteryhaugh - Bewshaugh - Cat Cairn - Purdon Pike - Butteryhaugh.

Start/Finish: Junction of the waymarked (cycle) forest road and the C200 at GR.628929, ½ mile/0.8 km south of Kielder village. Car parking at Kielder village or the car park at Bakethin.

Type of walk: *Although this 5½ mile/8.8 km walk passes through established forest, the route is open and never claustrophobic; providing, in a height gain of 820ft/250m, extensive views of the surrounding hills and, in the opinion of many, the finest views of Bakethin and Kielder Water. Graded 3, due to the summit traverse of Purdon Pike, the walk is mainly via forest roads and grassy rides visiting the habitat of the extinct Kielder wildcats plus a unique Tynedale "Flow". Walking shoes/boots are needed for this rewarding 3 hour walk. The following route description, covering a preponderance of forest tracks, may seem to be a constant series of repetitive commands. My apologies if it makes dull reading; thankfully, the walking is never so.*

Accommodation and refreshments: in/around Kielder village.

THE WALK: From the C200 highway, enter the waymarked forest road by the sign "Forestry Vehicles Only", on a gentle incline south-west. Wind past a water tank (Kielder Village Water Supply, May 1954) on the left before swinging right, i.e. north-west, at the waymarked fork (the forest track ahead is our return route). Continue making height with the road, north and west to the crossroads, where fine sightings of Deadwater Fell to the north can be enjoyed. Our route is due west over the crossroads before swinging left to below the distinctive outcrop of Cat Cairn on the right. The road loops around Cat Cairn, and tracks coming in on our left should be ignored, i.e. at the two forks take the right branch each time to ascend north alongside the higher reaches of the grass and heather-clad outcrops of Cat Cairn.

This prominent outcrop is not man-made, but is a typical Kielder sandstone crag, reputed to have been the last known home to the Kielder wildcats. Now extinct in this part of the country, these wildcats roamed and hunted on the fells of Upper Tynedale. The flat-topped boulders of Cat Cairn provide a fine viewing platform.

After a careful inspection and an appreciation of the views, continue north over a feeder burn and north-west for ¼ mile/0.4 km to a narrow ride on the left, along which an unused grass-clad track takes us south-west through the confines of a dark stand of spruce to the open lands of Purdon Pike Flow.

Flow, a Scots word for the unique morasses or mires found on the high ground in upper Tynedale; in addition to this flow, examples can be found at Drowning Flow (Walk 16) and Hobb's Flow (Walk 17). These Internationally Significant Protected Border Mires/Flows, devoid of trees, contain rare plant species and were in fact noted by that intrepid traveller, Sir Walter Scott, in the early 1800s.

The traverse southwards of this heather, tussock and cotton grass wilderness is assisted by a metre-wide pathway which eases navigation and ankle strain. Ahead, once the skyline is reached, the path leads to a lone pine standing alongside the remains of an unusual watch tower, an ideal spot for refreshment and a long draught of dramatic scenery over the two reservoirs below.

Several of these early Forestry Commission octagonal watch towers, fashioned in the style of garden pergolas, were sited on the fell tops as look-out fire towers. Today, little remains on Purdon Pike except the foundations and a stalked octagonal table (handy for your refreshment break), although the extensive views of Bakethin and Kielder Water remain.

Leave this treeless summit south with the path, entering the spruce at the angled south-eastern corner and continue south to join a forest road.

Descend south and east, passing an incoming road from the left, to a distinct crossroads; take the road left, i.e. north, ¼ mile/0.4 km to a forked junction. Swing right, gradually descending east, ignoring the incoming track on the left, to the T-junction; roe deer are attractive and interesting animals to observe from the nearby rides. Go sharp left, i.e. north-north-west, on a forest road for one arrow-straight mile/1.6 km, with fine views north-east and north of Kielderhead Moor, The Border Line and Deadwater Fell. By the third burn crossing, at GR.622926, a winding twin-track road and gully enter from the right. Ascend north-north-west with the curving "main road" flanked by forest for 240 paces to reach a boulder stone and waymarked ride on the right. Leave the forest road north-east for a more secluded continuation of our journey via the needle-strewn path in forest fringes of the ride, a short up and down ride of some 400yds/m north-east, to meet a grassy track running with the deer fence. Turn right, descending south and east with the curving track, opening up and presenting fine vistas to the right of the glistening waters of Kielder water beyond Bakethin weir, before joining our outward route at the waymark. From there it is but a short walk to the gated (invariably open) junction with the C200 highway.

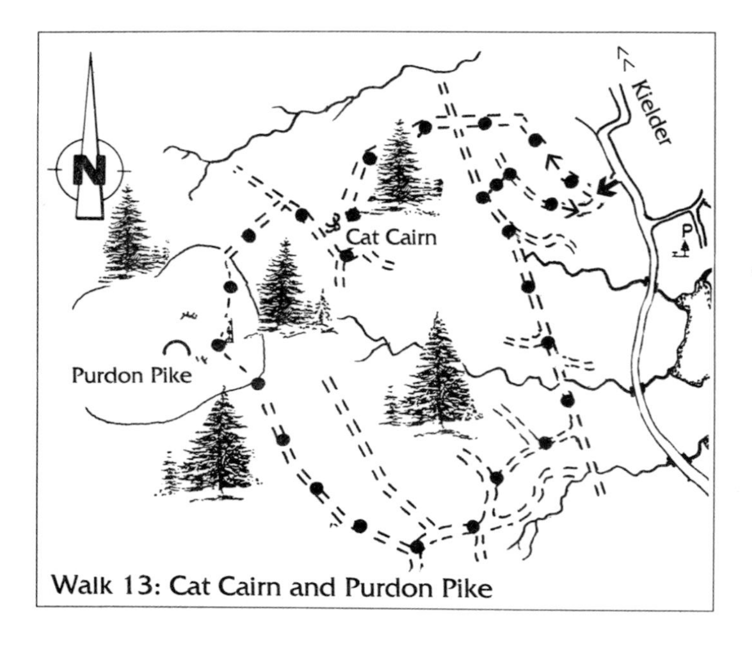

Walk 13: Cat Cairn and Purdon Pike

CHAPTER 3

THROUGH FOREST TO FELL: Where Eagles Fly

A selection of challenging and rewarding walks for the enthusiast, six circular, one linear. Walks that, with the exception of the Kielder Water Circuit Challenge Walk, rise high through the forests to the airy fells beyond. Fells that bear the marks of man and passing time, fells that generously reward the walker with evocative solitude and the sights and secrets of nature. Such rewards are, however, not given lightly to the searcher, for whilst the forest sections are mainly on forest tracks and recognisable paths, the open fells may have to be traversed in wilderness conditions; at best on narrow sheep traces, at worst through virgin heather or sections of black peat and mossy mires.

To ensure maximum enjoyment it is essential to be prepared:-

1) Wear the right gear, especially footwear, to keep you warm and dry in winter and cool in summer.

2) Have the ability to read a map and compass, in addition to taking this guide.

3) Take a supply of water and high energy snacks.

4) Leave a note of your route, colour of clothing and ETR (estimated time of return).

5) Do not forget camera and binoculars.

ADVENTURES FOR THE ENTHUSIAST - At a Glance

More fell than forest, Walk 14 reveals castle ruins, cadger's crossings, a sandstone gorge with surging linn; whilst Walk 15 provides an airy fell and drovers' approach to the delights of Tarset Burn, with a pleasing forest return to Falstone. Walk 16 is a north/south linear walk through forest and over high fell that will test the resolve and stimulate the senses, in particular the visual. A toll road is taken on Walk 17, by two of Kielder's finest burns, to Bloody Bush and Larriston Fells high above Liddesdale. Kielder Castle marks our starting point for Walks 18 and 19; 18 ascends to Devil's Lapful and Three Pikes providing views of the wind-blown heights, in addition to travelling 2,000 years through time. Walk 19 "Bundle & Go's" to the Border Line, via a covenanter's cave and Peel Fell to Kielder Stane, the Border's largest post office. Listed as a challenge walk, Walk 20 is just that, covering 26 miles around the shores of Kielder Water and Bakethin Reservoir, a journey that is guaranteed to invigorate the soul and benumb the body.

Bloody Bush Toll Bar

WALK 14:

BY JERRY'S LINN TO OPEN FELL

Chirdon Burn Bridge - Dally Castle - Cadger Ford - The Bower - Allerybank - Jerry's Linn (Chirdon Burn) - Cairnglastenhope - Whitchester - Snabdaugh Moor - Chirdon Burn Bridge.

Start/Finish: Layby south-east of Chirdon Burn Bridge (GR.783849). 1½ miles/2.4 km south of Lanehead and 5 miles/8 km west of Bellingham on a narrow unclassified road.

Type of walk: *A 10½ mile/16.8 km circular journey offering an "à la carte" of Kielder experiences rarely enjoyed in one walk. Serene and savage scenery, by Chirdon Burn to thundering Jerry's Linn, will delight the walker. Graded 3, though should the final ¼ mile/0.4 km to Jerry's Linn be attempted by scrambling alongside and over Chirdon Burn a Grade 4 would apply, the way is by country lanes, cart and forest tracks, grassy paths and for Grade 4, burnside boulder scrambles. Waymarked for the final miles, the central forest sections require careful navigation and correct footwear, thus adding to the adventure factor; the overall ascent of 630ft/192m is gradual. Journey time 5 hours.*

Accommodation and refreshments: in/around Bellingham or Falstone.

THE WALK: Start by crossing the arched stone bridge (circa 1821) over Chirdon Burn turning immediately left to the pillared gates of Birks.

A short distance north stands the isolated church of Greystead, erected by Greenwich Hospital in 1818 when dividing Simonburn parish.

Circle the mansion house and pass Birks cottages west and south-west to rejoin Chirdon Burn for a tree-lined walk to Dally House, Mill and Castle.

The ruined pele tower built in the 13th century by a Lindsay is a reminder that this area was once part of Scotland.

Continue west with the tree-lined lane and burn, to Cadger Ford and Chirdon sheltering below the sombre mass of Gallows Hill, a delightful walk in autumn when the dark conifer stands provide a harmonious backdrop for the searing reds and yellows of dying leaves, and rusting bracken glistening in the morning sun.

Cadger (a hawker/carrier) Ford is a crossing of some importance on an ancient east-west route travelled by Romans, reivers, drovers and cadgers; remarkably straight and traced by names on today's maps such as Watson's Walls, Cadger Ford and Drove Rigg.

With the open acres of Gallow Law on our left and the lane winding west-south-west we soon reach the tidy farm of The Bower, where a gated tarmac lane ascends south-west through pastures to a cattle grid into the forest.

At Bower, in the late 1620s, assorted Armstrongs stole 48 cows and oxen from William Charlton at the Bower, who recorded: "gat them all bake againe except sex."

100yds/m ahead at GR.750829 turn left, i.e. south, into a narrow grassy ride en route to Allerybank. (Note: The OS map shows a footpath running south-south-west, in reality it is a maze of junctions and bends).

The narrow ride leads south to a T-junction; turn right ascending south-south-west, passing an incoming ride on the right. Continue south to the next T-junction; take the right turn, i.e. south-west, on to a well-worn moss and grass twin-track that eventually emerges on to a minor forest track descending left to the one-time farmstead of Allerybank.

In the narrow rides where filtered light reaches the forest floor, many fungi flourish throughout autumn, such as the poisonous bright red Fly Agaric and the deadly Honey Fungus, a carrier of wet rot disease, and lethal to forest trees.

250 yds/m beyond the worn steps of the granary, a footbridge spans Chirdon Burn. Once across its pleasing waters, a faint overgrown trace winds right for 100yds/m to a crumbling walled enclosure, a "wigwam" symbol indicates this is one of Kielder Forest's 18 backpacking sites - details from Kielder Forest District Officer, Bellingham.

Ahead, Chirdon Burn eagerly dances out of its boulder-strewn gorge which can be reached via the south-western corner of the

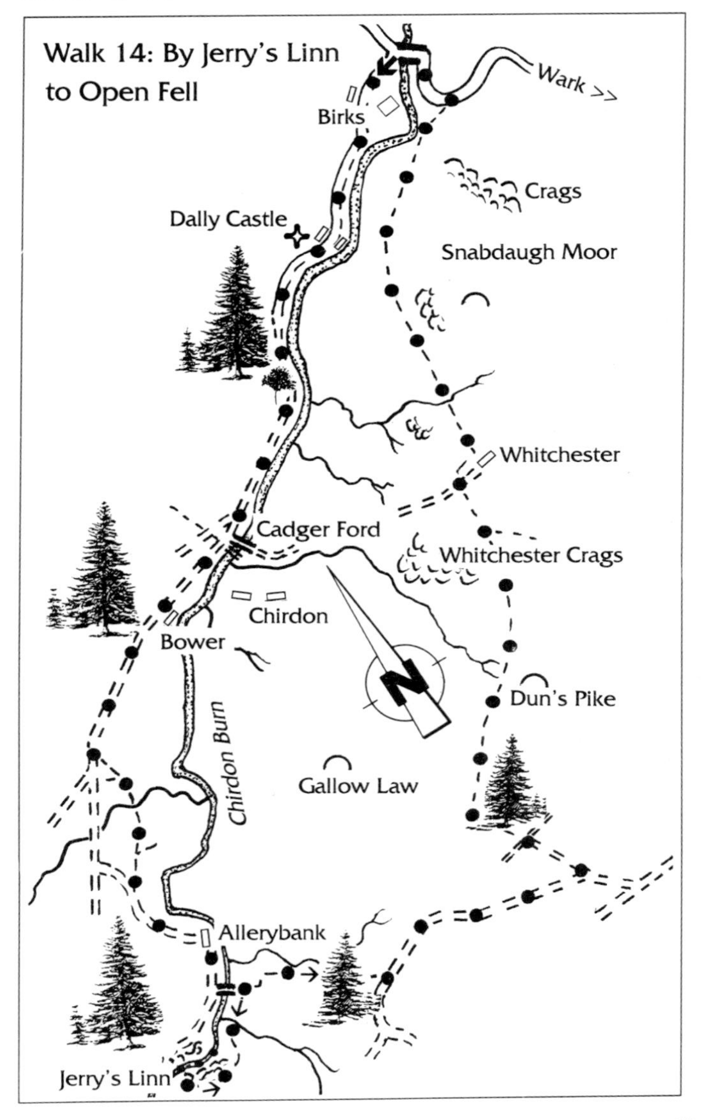
Walk 14: By Jerry's Linn to Open Fell
Wark >>
Birks
Crags
Dally Castle
Snabdaugh Moor
Whitchester
Cadger Ford
Whitchester Crags
Chirdon
Bower
Chirdon Burn
Dun's Pike
Gallow Law
Allerybank
Jerry's Linn

enclosure. Experienced scramblers can pursue the true right bank of the burn, others, for an easier path, should ascend left with the wall where a thin trace leads right, i.e. south-west, between fence and forest for an aerial view of thunderous Jerry's Linn cascading into the sandstone basin below.

For the scramble through the gorge, heed well the placement of your feet over slime-covered rocks and boulders by deep dark pools that swirl beneath the sandstone overhangs; all too soon the scrambling is over as Jerry's Linn, brown with peat stain, pours into its sandstone cauldron. The fell sandstone above the north bank can be scaled and the burn forded, enabling a return to the footbridge via the easier outward route south of the burn.

Ascend east to enter a forest ride at GR.749824 for a ½ mile/0.8 km spruce-lined walk south-east to Cairnglastenhope. At the first T-junction descend left to a crumbling dyke which is followed right, i.e. south-east. When the wall angles left, leave it and continue south-east in a narrow ride to a tiny clearing with a sprinkling of wall stones; 50yds/m beyond you reach a wide forest road and the open spaces of Cairnglastenhope. Ascend left with the road as it winds north and east for 1 mile/1.6 km to an intersection from the left; turn left on to this dirt track ascending for nearly ½ mile/0.8 km, through a ride to a small gate, to the open acres of Gallow Law and Chirdon Moor.

In 1314 tenants of Chirdon parish had the misfortune to be burdened with two landlords both claiming rent, resulting in 22 abandoned shielings.

Turn right on to a public bridleway alongside the forest fence, east-north-east, with the rushes, for 540yds/m to Dun's Pike and a small cairn on the ridge above, beyond the angled fence. This cairn and others waymark a footpath, north-north-east, over Chirdon Moor by Whitchester Crags to Whitchester Farm, 1 mile/1.6 km north.

An invigorating stretch providing extensive views of North Tynedale and an insight into the wildlife of the open moor. Just west of the cairned track a series of boundary stones lead to Whitchester Farm, each inscribed with a "W" on the east side and a "C" on the west side, signifying the Marches of Whitchester and Chirdon land over the open fell.

As Whitchester is approached, at the gate of three chains, a finger-post (marked "Cadgerford") directs the walker to the farm road below. A nearby waymarked (blue arrowhead) gate leads east through bracken to Whitchester Farm.

In the late 1800s and early 1900s the steading also housed a school, with pupils' names still visible on the woodwork.

From Whitchester the grassy way, north, to Chirdon Burn bridge is clearly and regularly waymarked by posted arrowheads; two arrowheads per post allows passage in either direction, for the 1½ miles/2.4 km traverse of Snabdaugh Moor.

"Snabduf", the local pronunciation, carries evidence of yesterday's coal mining activities below Hart Crags - grassed over spoil-heaps and gouged tracks made by heavy-laden pack ponies.

As the ridged route descends it passes through two waymarked gates into a flat pasture leading, via a solitary ash and an exit gate, to the final few yards left, along the lane, to Chirdon Burn Bridge end.

Walking in Sidwood

WALK 15:

FELL, FOREST, BASTLE & BURN

Falstone - Slaty Ford - Sidwood - Fire Tower - Hawkhope Hill - Falstone.

Start/Finish: Falstone (GR.724875), 1 mile/1.6 km east of Kielder Water and 10 miles/16 km west from Bellingham.

Type of walk: *Half fell, half forest, this 12 mile/19.2 km walk, with its optional extensions of 3¼ miles/5 km or 1¾ miles/3 km by Tarset Burn, traverses Reiver country. Ascending 1017ft/310m, it offers sweeping views of the North Tyne valley and the Border hills. Walking on roadside verges, grassy tracks, waymarked paths, forest roads and rides, the way is rich in plant and animal life with a picturesque picnic spot half way. This journey should be treated as a full day's leisurely adventure.*

Accommodation and refreshments: in Falstone and nearby Stannersburn.

THE WALK: Leave Falstone via the redundant rail bridge, swing right, i.e. south-west, passing the old station as the road rises to the owl-guarded Rectory gates.

The Border Counties Railway penetrated the North Tyne in 1862, running from Bellingham to Riccarton Junction. Later, the company was taken over by the North British, but is still affectionately known as the Counties Line. It perished in the great railways' plague of 1958.

Continue ascending by the strip of Scots pine, then at the rise turn left, i.e. north, on to a farm road (signposted "Border Counties Ride").

At a solitary stone gatepost the way swings right, i.e. east-north-east, for a 1½ mile/2.4 km high, wide and handsome hike above the North Tyne, framed by the craggy fells of Chirdon and Whitchester Moors and Shitlington and Thorneyburn Commons, where one's only companions, apart from the ubiquitous sheep, are the curlew, peewit, meadow pipit, stonechat, singing lark and crowing cock. This waymarked gated way eventually descends to Slaty Ford, where

Reservoir and tower on the Belling Walk

Whickhope Anchorage from Elf Kirk

On the way to Hindhope Linn

Duchess Bridge

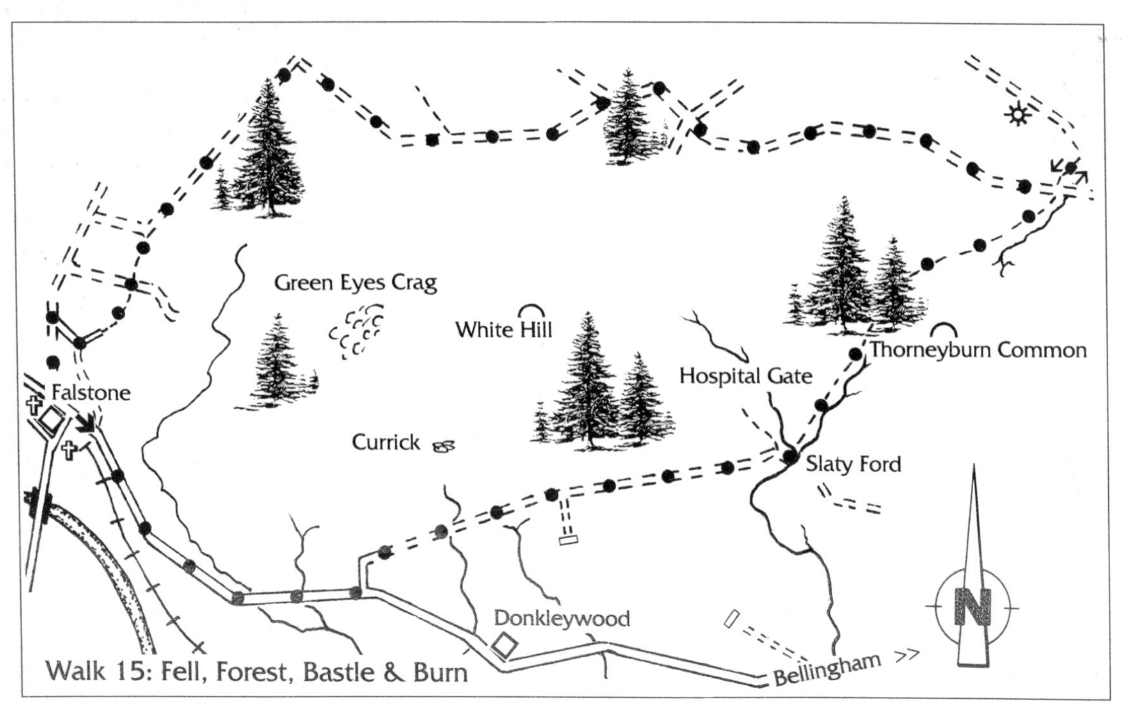

Walk 15: Fell, Forest, Bastle & Burn

Thorney Burn slides over slabs of water-worn rock. Just prior to the ford turn left, i.e. north-east, to ascend for ½ mile/0.8 km on a farm track close by Thorney Burn to the conifers of Sidwood. At the elbowed fence, pass through the gate to a thin path betwixt trees and dyke to reach the next angle. Take the third ride from the left, i.e. north-east, to enter the Sidwood maze.

The directions to Sidwood, through dark alleys of spruce, are of necessity precise, and walkers are advised to follow them to the letter.

Ascend the ride, north-east, at the first junction swing left, i.e. north, for 30yds/m then turn sharp right into a narrow and clarty ride. Continue to a crossroads (ride right and large cleared strip left), take the ride ahead, descending a faint grassy path. When next a crossroads is met, a glimmer of hope with a glimpse of Belling Rigg and Great Dodd, carry on ahead descending to meet and cross a sandy forest road. Enter the opposite ride where a wider path winds down to the idyllic setting of Sidwood Cottage, car park and picnic area.

For those of an inquisitive nature and a strong stride, there are two fascinating extensions detailed on the information board. The "Reiver's Trail" offers two short circular walks of 3¼ miles/5 km (see Walk 11) or 1¾ miles/3 km, waymarked yellow and red, by Tarset Burn visiting the bastles (fortified farmhouses) of Woodhouse, Waterhead, Shilla Hill, Bog Head and Black Middens.

Ascend from Sidwood Car Park into the conifers on the outward path as far as the forest road. Turn right, i.e. west, on to this gentle road for 1½ miles/2.4 km. This open way presents fine views of the monument on Padon Hill to the north-east and to the north Reedswood Crag, Blackman's Law and Berrymoor Edge. At the next crossroads continue ahead following the road as it swings left through the trees to a fork. Ascend the sandy left fork, west, as it winds south-west and then west, in a pleasing avenue of foxgloves and handsome conifers. To the right a fire tower, beyond which the way descends to a stony forest road junction.

Forest roads, totalling hundreds of miles, are an essential part of timber production, as the presence of many sandstone quarries indicates.

Turn left, i.e. south-south-west, for a 2 mile/3.2 km swinging descent of 590ft/180m to Falstone. The road can be hard on tired feet; ignore side roads and continue on the wide forest road to a T-junction at GR.727882. Enter the descending ride opposite (waymarked

"APW") and continue south-south-west to the next forest road. Take the right fork to clear the conifers and meet the houses of Falstone.

To the west the massive dam of Kielder Water dominates the skyline, 44,000 million gallons of water, restrained by a dam 1250yds/ 1154m long containing 5.3 million cubic feet of material.

Falstone, derived from the Anglo-Saxon "Fausten" (a stronghold), built by Mowbray in the early 1300s, had two landlords at that time - one Scots and one English. No doubt times have not been easy, for marauding Scots burned what is now the Blackcock Inn in the early 1600s - note the fortified farmhouse of Falstone Farm. Today, this charming village is home to families whose property was submerged by Kielder Water in 1982.

Creatures of the Forest: the author and friends!

WALK 16:
THE EMBLEHOPE EXPERIENCE

Blakehopeburnhaugh - Forest Drive - Blackman's Law - Reedswood Crag - Emblehope Moor - Black Sike - Bog Head - Sidwood - Greenhaugh.

Start: Blakehopeburnhaugh Picnic Place/Car Park (GR.784002), 2 miles/3.2 km south from Byrness, just off the A68(T).

Finish: Greenhaugh (GR.795873), 4½ miles/7.2 km north-west of Bellingham.

Type of walk: *A linear walk of 12½ miles/20 km, as varied as it is rewarding, requiring return transport. Graded 4, it traverses all types of pathways and Tynedale terrain, including a little mild rock scrambling and girder walking, if desired. The views are evocative, the hands-on-history of reivers' tales is bloody, and wildlife abounds. Outdoor equipment and walking boots are essential, as are map and compass skills. Allow 6½/7 hours for the adventure; and unless you were born a masochist with webbed feet do not attempt the traverse in winter.*

Accommodation and refreshments: Holly Bush Inn, Greenhaugh; Bellingham; Blakehopeburnhaugh; Byrness.

THE WALK: Leave Blakehopeburnhaugh via the signposted Forest Drive, a quiet toll road, as it gently ascends west through an avenue of Norway spruce. As the majority of facilities provided by Forest Enterprise are free, walkers are not required to pay the toll. Continue west and west-south-west with the landscaped drive; just beyond the second track on the right a yellow arrowhead ("APW" - Alternative Pennine Way) leads south to Blackblakehope Picnic Place.

The monoculture stands of spruce, lining the drive, are now restructured with attractive broad-leaves such as silver birch and rowan.

Cross the peat-stained waters of Blakehope Burn by bridge,

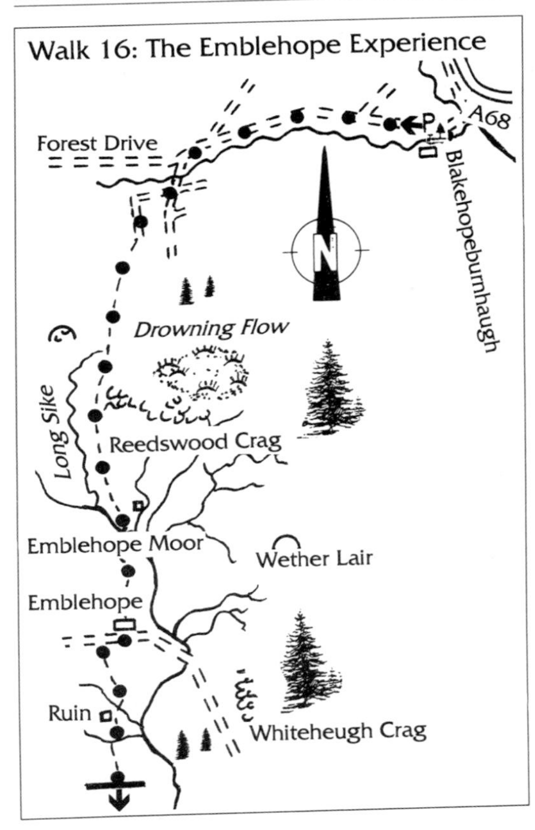

ascending south-west on a hard-core road, ignoring the road on the left, to take the waymarked dirt and grass track right as it drops into the forest. Follow this dwindling track west and south, between encroaching conifers, until it peters out. The way is now by a very slender, and in places wet, grass path, turning later to heather ascending through narrow silent rides, fortunately well way-marked, ("APW"). Wind south, south-west and south for 1 mile/1.6km, eventually breaking out via a stiled fence on to the extensive heather and moss-clad expanse of Emblehope Moor.

Emblehope Moor is a typical "BC" (Before Conifers) Northumbrian moor, exhibiting all the classic characteristics of its kind: sandstone crags, i.e. Reedswood Crag and Whiteheugh crag, mires/bogs known as flows, as in Drowning Flow (see Walk 13) and Ashy Bog, plus references to the ubiquitous sheep, i.e. Wether Lair - it is a habit of Cheviot sheep to move on to the tops as night approaches.

250yds/m west the domed crags of Blackman's Law provides a

marker for the journey south-south-west and south across the uncharted wastes to the western tip of Reedswood Crag. The way is rough, through heather, sphagnum, rushes and cotton grass, though not impossible, for the source and visible gully of Long Sike act as a guide for the ½ mile/0.8 km tramp. Walk about 50ft/15m above the true left bank of Long Sike to the sculptured stones, from which an aid to the next stage can be seen to the south. Two round, stone sheep stells stand out, and several narrow sheep traces wind south from Reedswood Crag to the right-hand stell. As the stell is reached, a twin track can be distinguished running south and waymarked (bridleway) posts miraculously appear leading to a wooden bridge below the tin-roofed Reedswood Fold.

Heathers and heaths inhabit the higher drier areas; cotton grass and deer sedge mark the sphagnum bogs, where a few gems such as the round-leaved sundew, bog asphodel, andromeda, crowberry and cloudberry can be found. Glacial deposits (drumlins) pimple the moor and the silence is broken only by the distinctive cries of grouse and whaup.

Over the bridge the waymarks plot a course through a sea of rushes, rising to the timber stands that herald Emblehope Farm.

During the 1640s, mosstroopers (Armstrongs) took sixty cows and oxen and eleven horses and mares from Emblehope.

Once through the farm gates, turn right on to a tarmac road, and with the trees swing left, i.e. south, on to the open moor. A distinct twin-track continues south, via several gates and a footbridge over Smallhope Burn, to a derelict shieling by the forest's edge; on the eastern skyline the distinctive cliffs of Whiteheugh Crag can be picked out. Beyond the shieling a ruined bridge over Hunter's Burn offers a tightrope crossing on two slim and unstable girders to a gated, waymarked forest ride; for safety's sake walk 25yds/m east to a tapered angle in the burn that can be cleared with an energetic leap.

The next mile/1.6 km is south through forest, by narrow ride and harvested stand, well waymarked ("APW"/Bridleway) on narrow needle-strewn paths, passing the grass-grown stones of a ruined Long House, with accompanying spring, before emerging to unexpected views over Tarset valley, of Belling Rigg and Hareshaw Common. A forest road, our first since Blakehope Burn, terminates our affair with the Alternative Pennine Way; turn left descending south-east with the road for 1½ scenic miles/2.4 km to a bridleway waymark leading left, i.e. east, through the trees to a clearing with the

Long House and Bastle of Bog Head by the banks of Tarset Burn.

"Barty's Pele" (a bastle), home in the 1600s to Bartholomew Milburn, a man of his time, who removed Scotsman's heads whilst recovering or replacing his sheep (see Walk 11).

Continue south-east with Tarset Burn before leaving the trees and ascending south-west to Shilla Hill, site of the crumbling bastle of Starr Head. From here a grassy track leads south to join the forest road to Waterhead cottage, site of the 15th/16th century fortified farm-house of Waterhead. Once across the road bridge swing right with

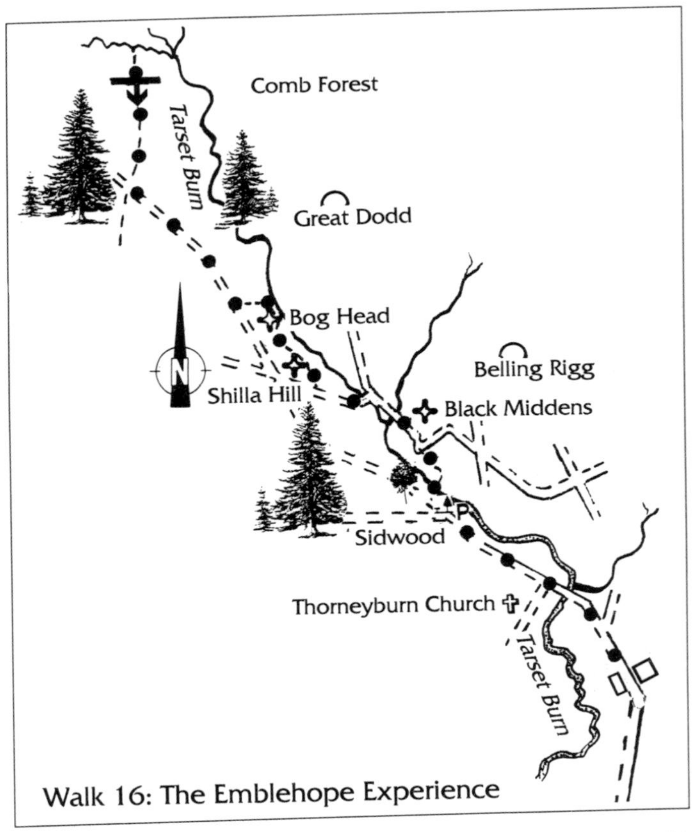

Walk 16: The Emblehope Experience

the waymarks to the ford, bridge and footbridge over Black Burn to the clearly visible restored bulk of Black Middens.

Black Middens is a bastle with an adjoining 18th century long house, in which man and beast lived under the same roof and used the same door; life in Tarset valley was not for the faint-hearted!

Walk east with the road to the U-bend, and at the waymarked gate a pasture path winds south with the fence to a footbridge over Tarset Burn. Cross and turn left, through the rustic gate, on to a delightful path winding with the tree-lined burn to emerge at Sidwood's white cottage, car park and picnic place. A place of sylvan peace and tranquillity, pleasing on the eye and a credit to the foresters, and a possible journey's end. For those who wish to continue for the final 2 miles/3.2 km it provides a spot to rest and ponder.

Several alternatives for the walk to Greenhaugh present themselves, and as no doubt you have had your fill of gates, stiles and waterlogged pastures, the most relaxing and scenically rewarding route is via the narrow lane leading south-east and south to Greenhaugh.

Walk south-east with the lane, and as the conifers thin, the forest finally ends at the curves by Redheugh, the way now lined with avenues of fine stone dyke as it approaches Tarset Burn bridge and Burnmouth.

On the right hand skyline stands Thorneyburn Church, erected in the early 19th century by Greenwich Hospital when dividing the unwieldy parish of Simonburn.

Beyond Burnmouth ignore the fork to the left and begin the final ½ mile/0.4 km into the hamlet of Greenhaugh, ahead the widening valley of Tarset as it spills and blends into the green and distant acres of upper Tynedale.

WALK 17:
TO BLOODY BUSH TOLL and LARRISTON FELLS

Lewisburn Picnic Area - The Forks - Akenshaw - Bloody Bush - Larriston Fells - Buck Burn - Lewis Burn - Lewisburn Picnic Area.

Start/Finish: Lewis Burn Car Park/Picnic Area (GR.636896), ½ mile west from C200 and 3 miles/4.5 km south-south-east of Kielder village.

Type of walk: *13 miles/20.8 km, waymarked in places, through wide corridors of conifers with a gradual height gain of 1024ft/312m on to the purple summit of Larriston Fells 1680ft/512m. Graded 4, this historic route is by forest tracks, grassy roads, winding forest burns and narrow trods over heather and hag. A walk of 6½ hours, rich in wildlife with many photographic opportunities.*

Accommodation and refreshments: in/around Kielder and Leaplish.

THE WALK: From the car park via the Exit sign, turn right on to the forest road, running south-west with the picturesque Lewis Burn and its fringing ponds, to The Forks (two cottages). Cross the solid stone bridge ahead following the right fork to the confluence of the Lewis and Akenshaw Burns. Continue left with the tree-lined waters of Akenshaw Burn to cross a second bridge, the tree-lined road continues west-north-west for 1 mile/1.6 km to a third stone bridge prior to Akenshaw Cottages.

To the left stands the crumbling single arch of "Oakenshaw" Brig, a bridge, and adjacent toll-keeper's cottage, mentioned on the Toll Bar at Bloody Bush as the place for toll payments. Originally, there was an "O" in Oakenshaw, lost through time, for now OS maps list burn, brig and cottages as"Akenshaw". The toll road and brig were used to transport coal from the nearby workings via Bloody Bush to Dinlabyre in Liddesdale.

Ascend west-north-west with the forest road contouring Buck Fell; ignoring tracks to the left, pass a sandstone quarry to cross the deep-gouged channel of Buck Burn. Here the road narrows as it continues west-north-west to reach the restored bridge over Black Knowe Burn.

Completed in 1992, the bridge bears an original plaque, stating it was built in 1828 for Sir J E Swinburn. Keep an eye open for several crumbling high-arched bridges carrying the toll road before Bloody Bush.

From this point the track underfoot deteriorates to a damp grassy path, narrowing as it approaches Bloody Bush, the Toll Bar Stone and the open expanse of Larriston Fells. Bloody Bush marks the site of a long-forgotten skirmish.

The Toll Bar on the Border Line, a 14ft stone pillar with a base 5½ foot square whose inset states: "The Tolls are to be paid at Oakenshaw Bridge to Sir J E Swinburn, Capheaton, and Wm Oliver Rutherford, Dinlabyre. 1d per horse and cart, Other Horses 3d, Cattle 1d each, Calfs, Sheep and Swine ½p each."

In 1862 the Counties Railway penetrated Tynedale and connected with the Waverley Line at Riccarton Junction, marking the demise of the Bloody Bush Toll Road. Bloody Bush and surrounding landmarks were visited by that insatiable traveller and romantic Sir Walter Scott during his Liddesdale Raids when collecting song, verse and legend.

The fell path, wet in places, climbs steadily west-north-west into Scotland for ¾ mile/1.2 km to the hard road below the radio mast. Walk north to the mast and beyond venture forth, north-east for ½ mile/0.8 km across peat and heather, via a gate between dyke and fence to the cairn-scattered summit of Larriston Fells.

A seat in the "Gods" provides compelling views of both sides of the Border, in particular into Liddesdale. The three untidy cairns west of the summit were mentioned in 1660, as the "Three Grey Lads" astride the Border Line; Scotland appears to have expanded by ½ mile since those days. Below, alongside Liddel Water, the army of Bonnie Prince Charlie passed by in 1745 bound for Carlisle and beyond; the Prince spending the night at Larriston, home of the Elliots.

From the trig point traverse the pathless wilderness due east for ½ mile/0.8 km to the right angle in the Border fence and forest edge, (the treeless summit of Purdon Pike is a good marker). Descend east with the broken dyke on a grassy path to the hard-core forest road below - watch out for grazing roe deer.

Turn right, i.e. south-east, on to the welcome surface of the road,

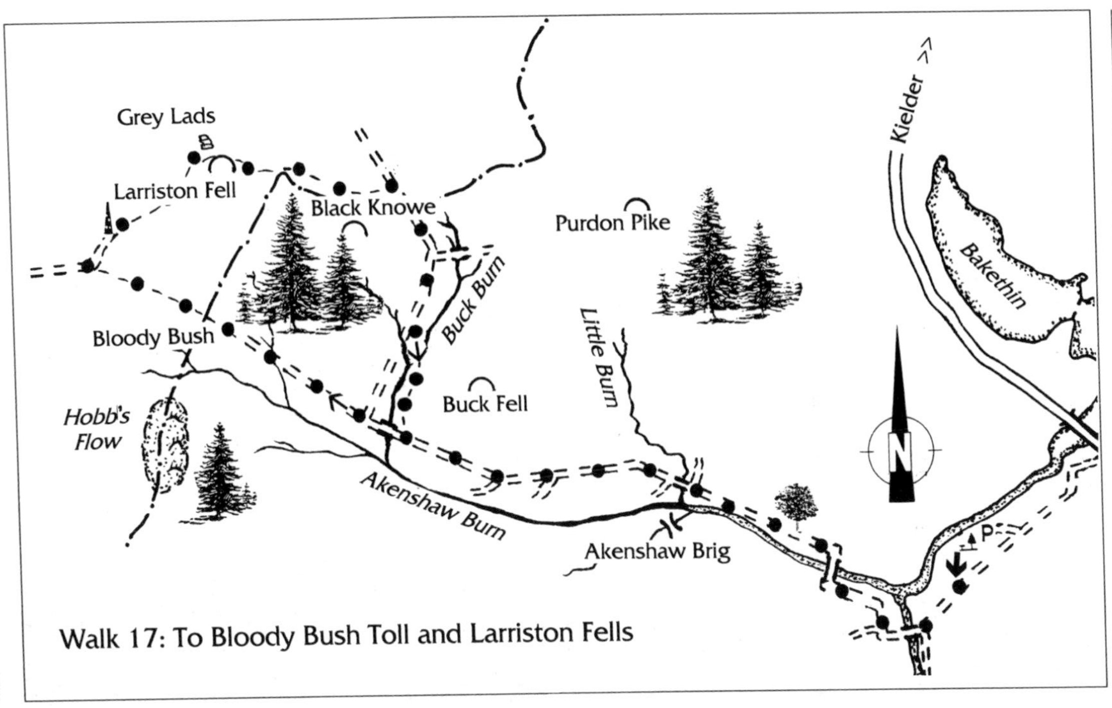

Walk 17: To Bloody Bush Toll and Larriston Fells

descending between the ranks of silent conifers to a fork; swing right, south, for ½ mile/0.8 km to a waymark on the left 60yds/m beyond a feeder burn, at GR.589907. Turn sharp left into the conifers on a narrow ride, and after 50yds/m swing right, i.e. south-south-east, with moss and heather underfoot. At the next junction turn right to join tree-smothered Buck Burn. Descend south with the burn for 200yds/m to a clearing above the outward Bloody Bush Road. Descend left with the road, east-south-east, past Akenshaw on a broad-leaved tree-lined road for 1 mile/1.6 km to the stone bridge.

Do not cross the bridge, but leave the forest road to the left to join a delightful stepped and waymarked stretch along the north bank of Akenshaw Burn to Lewis Burn. Beyond, a footbridge is crossed for journey's end at Lewisburn Car Park/Picnic Area.

Forest cairn

WALK 18:
DEVIL'S LAPFUL and THREE PIKES: STONES OF LEGEND

Kielder Castle - "Skew-Arched" Viaduct - Devil's Lapful - Greys Pike - Three Pikes - Ridge End Burn - Kielder Burn - Kielder Castle.

Start/Finish: Kielder Castle Visitor Centre (GR.633935).

Type of walk: *A circular walk of 9 miles/14.4 km, rising 804ft/245m by forest and fell to the elevated isolation of Greys Pike and Three Pikes. Revealing seldom seen sights of lonely crags and the shimmering waters of Bakethin and Kielder Water, before descending with two of Kielder's picturesque burns. Graded 3, this 4/4½ hour journey is via forest roads, waymarked paths, heathery ways and burnside banks by forest fringes. A walk of scenic excellence, displaying striking examples of man's presence from prehistoric to Victorian times.*

Accommodation and refreshments: (and camp site) in/around Kielder village.

THE WALK: From Kielder Castle walk south past the Anglers Arms and over the bridge, turning left at the road junction; 15yds/m beyond cross the road and veer right on to the tree-lined way known as the Duke's Drive. A narrow driveway alongside the infant North Tyne from Kielder viaduct to Kielder Castle, used by the Dukes of Northumberland on their sporting visits to Kielder. The drive runs south-west to Bakethin Car Park where a stepped path leads on to the now defunct Border Counties Railway. Turn left to reach the elevated, grassy deck of this unique Tynedale viaduct, known to all as the "Skew Arched" Viaduct.

Built in 1862 at a cost of £4,572, the viaduct spans 120yds/m, rising 55ft/17m. Its angled arches and supporting pillars are positioned obliquely to the direction of the deck, thus presenting the line of least resistance to the seasonal spates of the turbulent North Tyne.

Immediately south of the viaduct descend left on a stepped path through an open forest to a road. Cross into Camp Rig clearing, via a waymarked wicket gate, north-north-east, for 200yds/m to an ancient homestead, an Iron Age/Roman settlement of ¼ acre with a single banked earthwork.

Continue east into the forest, ignoring all side paths, to cross a second forest road on to a narrow waymarked path through bracken and grass, rising east-north-east to yet another forest road (forked). Cross at the fork and continue east-north-east with the ride to the next forest road. At this point turn right, i.e. south, for 250yds/m to a waymark on the right indicating a small clearing containing the Devil's Lapful.

This rash of boulders is a Stone Age burial cairn positioned on the 1,000ft/300m contour, 60yds long and 13yds wide, and dated approximately 2,000 BC. One of several on these fells, now sorely mutilated by "robbing holes".

Return north to the waymarked ride, swing right, i.e. east-north-east, zigzagging with the forest fringes for ¾ mile/1.2 km and ascending left to the fire tower and Forsyth's Cairn on Mount Common. Continue east with the tracked forest ride to Greys Pike; underfoot heather and blaeberry. Once clear of the conifers ascend to a line of rotting posts running north to the trig point of Greys Pike, at 1460ft/445m the walk's highest point. Proceed north with the posts to its twin top, where there are impressive views north-east of the Border wilderness. The posts run out at this point and a clear path takes the walker north-north-east/north-east for 1 mile/1.6 km through heather, tussock and rocky outcrop along the elevated ridge to the cairns known as the Three Pikes.

The Three Pikes are of unusual construction, 2yds/m high, triangular in section and outline, built on fell sandstone outcrops they consist mainly of triangular stone slabs. Two others, identical in every way, can be seen on Windlestraw Law 38 miles to the north. They remain a mystery as they do not relate to elevation, boundaries or burial sites; nearby, a fourth cairn, is a rogue of modern inferior construction.

From the cairns descend north-north-east to the forest edge where a track drops steeply north-east/north, passing a sheep stell, to the footbridge over the surging Ridge End Burn as it hurries by from Oh Me Edge.

The remaining miles are a burnside delight. Do not cross the bridge but follow Ridge End Burn basically west along its true left bank as it

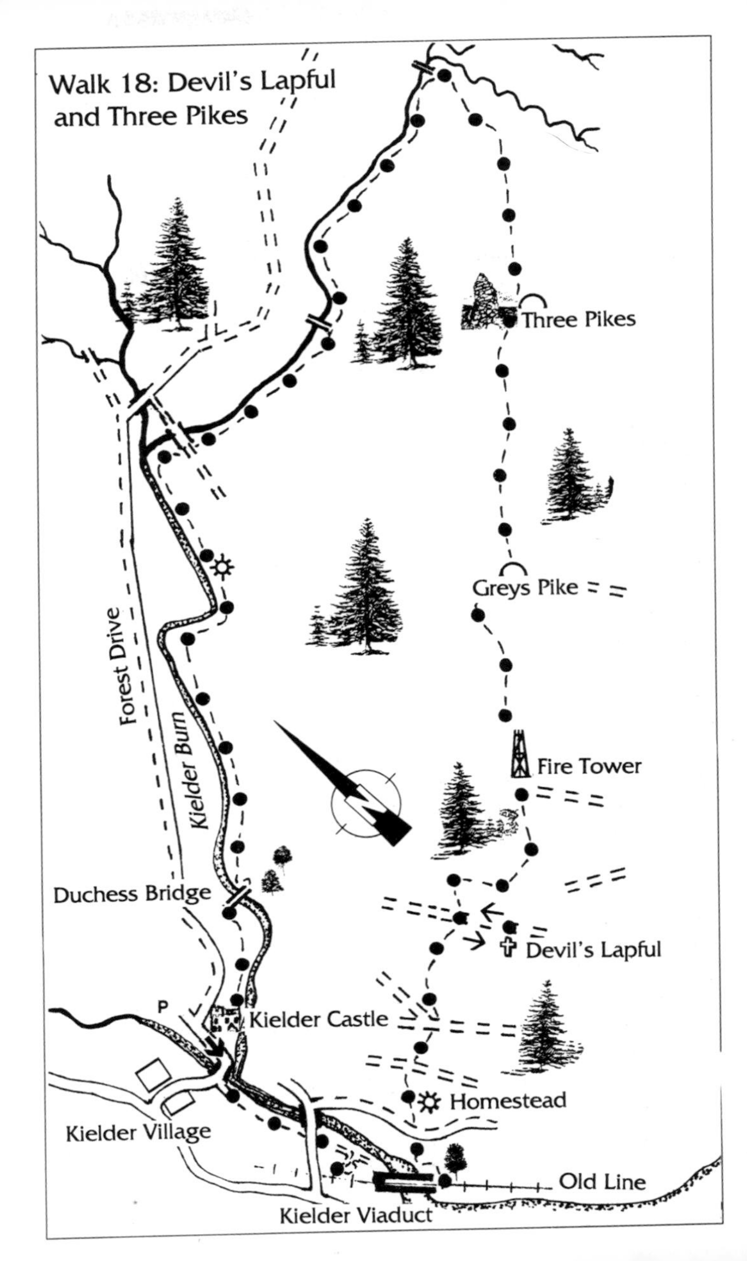
Walk 18: Devil's Lapful
and Three Pikes
Three Pikes
Greys Pike
Fire Tower
Forest Drive
Kielder Burn
Duchess Bridge
Devil's Lapful
P
Kielder Castle
Homestead
Kielder Village
Old Line
Kielder Viaduct

hurries through open fell and by forest fringe. After 1 mile/1.6 km, at the next footbridge, enter the forest left by a waymarked stile and continue with the burnside spruce to emerge by the junction with Kielder Burn.

In addition to the many wild flowers, look out for stately herons, so gracefully lethal to small fish and frogs; also predatory goosanders, a saw billed duck, the drake almost white, and cheeky dippers, a small bobbing bird who walks under water searching for molluscs, tadpoles and larvae.

Cross the road to the waymarked true left bank of the Kielder Burn south-west for 2 miles/3.2 km to the Duchess Bridge, a small hump-backed bridge over Kielder Burn that enabled the Duchess of Northumberland to drive her coach from the castle to meet the incoming sportsmen.

Cross the bridge and the meadow by a distinct path to Kielder Castle, passing en route a gauging station, fish hatchery and salmon cauld, Border Park RFC where the first international soccer match with the auld enemy was held, and an adventure playground containing a giant wooden xylophone.

Skew-Arched Bridge

WALK 19:
"BUNDLE AND GO" TO KIELDER STANE

Kielder Castle - Ravenshill Moor (Peden's Cave) - Deadwater Fell - Mid Fell - Kielder Stane - Peel Fell - Deadwater - Bellsburnfoot - Kielder Castle.

Start/Finish: Kielder Castle Visitor Centre (GR.633935).

Type of walk: *A circular 12½ miles/20 km trek, through forest and over purple fell, on forest roads, moorland trails and disused railways, the walk ascends 2064ft/629m, with an average walking time of 6¾ hours. Hill walking equipment, especially footwear, is essential, with map/ compass skills needed in poor visibility. A Grade 4 traverse of wild and lonely uplands, rich in history and home to a variety of fell and forest wildlife, visiting en route the massive Kielder Stane and Kielder's finest grandstand, Peel Fell. Don't forget the camera.*

Accommodation and refreshments: in/around Kielder village.

THE WALK: Leave Kielder Castle for Castle Wood Car Park, exiting at the north-west corner through deciduous trees, (listen for the chaffinch and the drilling of woodpeckers), to join a broad forest road. Turn left, i.e. west-north-west, for ¾ mile/1 km, passing Ravenshill to reach a rough track on the right; ascend north for ½ mile/0.8 km to a stile at the fence (GR.628952). Ahead, crags on the skyline of Ravenshill Moor indicate the rock, Fell Sandstone, of Deadwater Fell, Mid Fell and Peel Fell. Left, Lightpipe Sike rushes by, and overhead the curlew's plaintive cry.

Cross the heather and tussock-clad moor, north, on faint sheep traces above a crumbling sheep stell to the centre of the crag, where a stunted tree clings precariously to a wind-worn overhang close by Peden's Cave (GR.628957).

This small cave provided shelter for preacher Alexander (Sandy)

Peden, a Scottish covenanter driven over the Border by Bonnie Dundee's Dragoons in the mid-1600s, who held prayer meetings on the surrounding hills.

Ascend left of the cave to the fence, passing an electric pole; proceed north by the fence to reach a gate (GR.628959) on to a rough road ascending north to the summit of Deadwater Fell, crowned with outcrops of Fell Sandstone, assorted receivers, transmitters, beacons and balls. The top offers fine views of the jinking North Tyne Valley that cradles Bakethin and Kielder Reservoirs.

Descend east on a thin path between the new road and the fence on to Deadwater Moor. Not the easiest section, but on a day when grasses gently ebb and flow and the only sound is the skylark's song, then this exhilarating ridge walk is not to be missed. At first glance it appears as a desert of peat and heather; it can however be traversed with ease and safety using the metal/wood fence posts as waymarks. A dark lochan lurks left; ascend north-north-east with the posts for ½ mile/0.8 km to Mid Fell, on which an untidy cairn marks a tumulus/ burial mound of Iron Age chieftains.

Continue north, on a peaty path by a nail-embedded post on the skyline to reach a large wooden post 250yds/m below Peel Fell ridge. This strainer post indicates the Border Line. Turn right, i.e. north-east, descending with the fence posts over open fell on to a peaty pathway above Kielder Stone Cleugh. After ¾mile/1.2 km the colossus that is the Kielder Stone explodes into view.

The Kielder Stone is 1,500 tons of sandstone, 26ft x 50ft x 30ft, standing four square on the Border Line. Centuries ago during the troubles it served as a cross border Post Box; messages/letters were left in its rocky cracks for later collection. It also bears the Border Mark, "N" "D" (D reversed), "N" signifies the Duke of Northumberland, "D" the Douglas Estate. Nearby Kielderhead Moor is a designated Site of Special Scientific Interest (SSSI) with a wide range of moorland plant communities; particularly sensitive during the breeding season (March - July), when visitors are requested to keep to the public footpaths and waymarked walks.

Return to the strainer post below Peel Fell, turning right with the fence to the insignificant grass-covered summit cairn of Peel Fell, where a much superior cairn stands to the north-west.

Peel Fell is: "A stern and dark-hued hill", her skirt now pine green, straddling the Border Line. To the east, the Cheviot and the distant North Sea, south-west the Solway Firth and the Lake District.

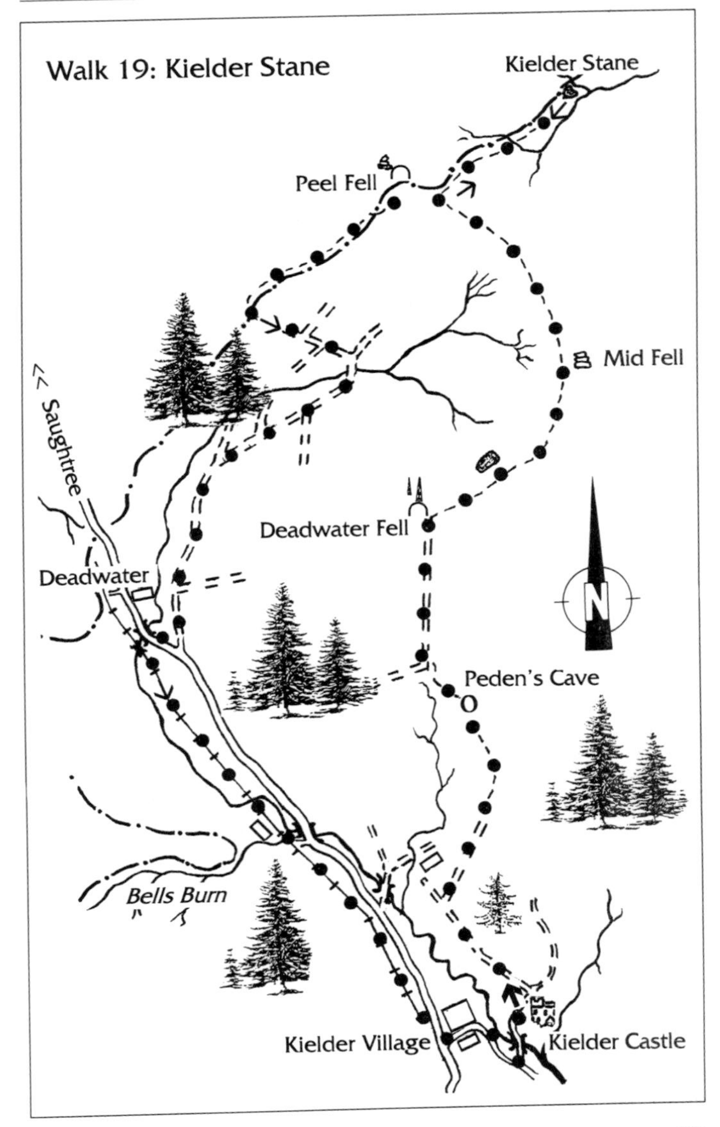
Walk 19: Kielder Stane
Kielder Stane
Peel Fell
Mid Fell
Saughtree
Deadwater Fell
Deadwater
Peden's Cave
Bells Burn
Kielder Village
Kielder Castle
N

Follow the posts north-west through peat black hags, swinging left to two rounded posts on the summit rim. Rejoin the Border fence by descending steeply south-west for ½ mile/0.8 km to the tree line.

Note Deadwater Corrie pimpled with stone outcrops, home to a small herd of feral goats, who produce their young in March and April.

Continue descending south-west *between the trees for 350yds/m to a waymarked grassy ride on the left.* Turn left, south-east, for 100yds/m to a tracked forest road; descend with the waymarked road, east-south-east, ignoring one road left and two right. When Deadwater Burn is crossed swing right, i.e. south-south-west, to the fork. Bear right, descend west then south-west for 1½ miles/2.4 km to the tarmac road south of Deadwater Farm.

Deadwater Fell, a watershed feeding Scotland and England has a watercourse at its foot so sluggish it appears undecided which way to flow, it was called "dead water" when compared with the hurrying water of the surrounding burns. Deadwater Farm was home in the 1640s to Janet Hann, a well-documented "Resetter", skilled at hiding, selling and disposing of "borrowed" cattle, sheep and goats.

Turn sharp right, i.e. north-north-west, on the roadside to the waymarked extremity of the left-hand trees. A faint path leads left, i.e. south-east, through the conifers by Deadwater Burn to a disused railway track over a two-arched bridge.

Border Counties Railway penetrated the North Tyne Valley in 1862, lived for 96 years and as the North British railway, died in 1958. Coal, from the North Tyne drift mines was carried to the Scottish border towns; it also provided fuel for lime-burning - note the ruined kilns west of Deadwater.

Turn left, i.e. south-east, on to the track for 2¾ miles/4.4 km passing Bell's Moor, Bellsburnfoot Cottage, and an old sawmill to Kielder village. But a short step remains, down Castle Drive to the village shop and finally, Kielder Castle.

WALK 20:

THE MARATHON - KIELDER WATER CIRCUIT CHALLENGE WALK.

Leaplish Lodge - Bull Crag - Tower Knowe - The Belling - Plashetts - Kielder Viaduct - Hawkhirst - Leaplish Lodge.

Start/Finish: Leaplish Waterside Park (Lodge)(GR.660878) on the south shore of Kielder Reservoir; 5½ miles/8.8 km south-south-east of Kielder village and 4½ miles/7.2 km west from Kielder Water Dam.

Type of walk: *The Kielder Circuit is a serious undertaking, providing the more ambitious walker with a strenuous full-day challenge. Obtain the Kielder Water Circuit Challenge Walk ('KWCCW') pack, for a modest fee, either at Leaplish Lodge or preferably in advance by telephoning Tower Knowe Visitor Centre, (01434) 240398, during normal working hours. It contains a map, walk details, a checkpoint card, pen and SAE. This enables the walker who completes the entire Challenge Walk in less than 12 hours, to apply for a Completion Pack comprising of certificate, exclusive T-shirt, car sticker and button badge. The KWCCW is not exclusively for the ambitious or sponsored walker, as it also caters for those who wish to complete the circuit by a series of shorter excursions, possibly linked by the Kielder ferry, Osprey.*

Graded 4, this fine adventure provides not only a surfeit of scenic pleasures but also a first-hand experience of forest and waterside flora and fauna and seldom-seen items of interest along the way. The KWCCW covers 26 miles/41.6 kms and can be done in 10/11 hours by fit and experienced walkers; I suspect the 26 listed miles are "Scots miles", i.e. 1,976½ yards per mile.

The circuit starts and finishes at Leaplish Lodge, where a time clock stamps your check point card (twelve

Checkpoints, each with a letter to be recorded). The way is well waymarked with posted "Otterprint" symbols; underfoot a varied mix of paths, from tarmac roads and prepared paths to sections of coarse wilderness walking along the north shore. Wear supportive footwear, with as rigid a sole as possible, along with clothing and equipment suitable for the prevailing weather conditions. High energy food, adequate water, a whistle and torch for emergencies and an OS Explorer Map should be carried. Remember to leave details of your intended route with friends or display them in your vehicle.

Accommodation and refreshments: Kielder, Leaplish (chalets) and Falstone; refreshments at Tower Knowe.

THE WALK: Once you have clocked-in at Leaplish Lodge you will be eager to be off into the trees via the car park and the "Shoreline footpath". Then go east by Leaplish Sike and avenues of venerable beech, planted 250 years ago as boundaries during the land enclosures of the period. Now they serve to mark the path to Checkpoint 1 by an Interpretive Panel - ½ mile/0.8 km from Leaplish. Well-waymarked, the path continues by the shore, passing Kielder water-ski club, to a short section of coarse walking as the dominant peninsula of Bull Crag approaches. A narrow grassy path rises to Otterstone Viewpoint.

The clutch of Scots pine and dolmen stone seats at Jubilee Plantation were laid out in 1977 to mark Queen Elizabeth's Silver Jubilee; enchanting views north-west leading to the ever-present Deadwater Fell.

Checkpoint 2 on Bull Crag is reached via a shoreline road, the old North Tyne Road into Scotland; east, as the crow flies, the dam is 1½ miles/2.4 km distant; on foot it is 6½ miles/10.4 km. Leave Bull Crag Picnic Place and a fine sandy track west, a favoured site of the shy goshawk, leading to an Otterprint waymark into the trees (miss it and you face an extra ¾ mile/1.2 km), and the C200 at Cranecleugh Bridge.

Cross the bridge south, then immediately turn left on to the track by Cranecleugh Burn. The waymarks on the right lead over a tussock-clad knowe to Whickhope Anchorage, cruiser clubhouse and jetties,

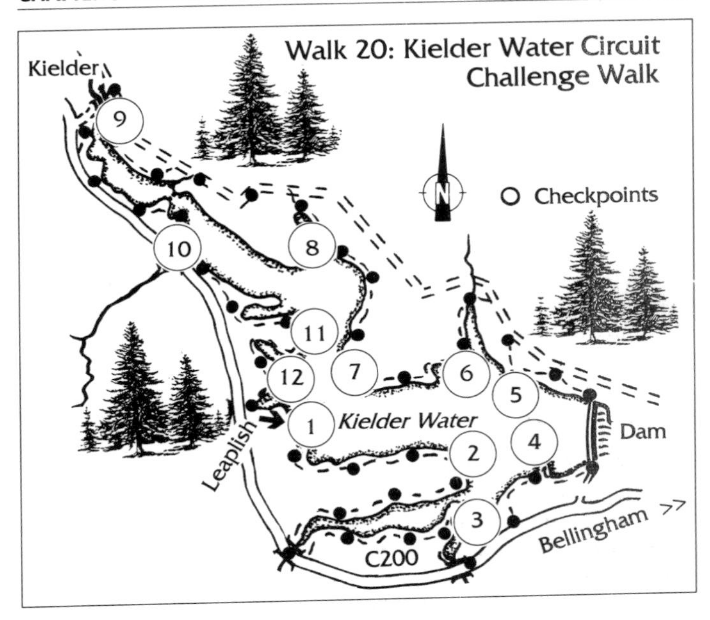

and beyond, the scenically pleasing Merlin Brae and Checkpoint 3.

The Interpretive Panel details the Dam, Tower Knowe, Elf Kirk, and Merlin Brae as a home for roe deer and red squirrel.

Once the water-ski school at Little Whickhope is passed, we emerge on to the C200 highway crossing Whickhope Burn Bridge. Follow the road, east and north-east for ¾ mile/1.2 km before plunging left at the waymark on to a well-defined, though in places stony, path through the scrubby approaches, by 19th century Shilburnhaugh drift mine and spoil heap, to Northumbrian Water's busy Tower Knowe Visitor Centre.

A small hump-backed bridge directs us north to a heather-and stone-clad cape peppered with plaques, cairns, an Interpretive Panel and a checkpoint.

A plaque here commemorates the 1976 Kielder Water Scheme and the panel details a Romano-British settlement.

Loop south and east before crossing the impressive Kielder Water Dam to Hawkhope Car Park/Picnic Place.

The dam, 1250yds/1154m long contains 5.3 million cubic feet of material and holds back 44,000 million gallons of water. It was at Hawkhope, in the 14th century, that an early forest worker murdered another with an axe.

Leave Hawkhope's comforts, with the Otterprint, for a delightful walk around The Belling as a starter for 10 miles/16 km of challenge along the north shore. A tranquil start beyond Gordon's Walls, ruins of a fortified farmstead, is through shady trees, yet within sight and sound of the dark-eyed inlets of Kielder Water. Belling peninsula, anchored to the north shore by a causeway, carries Checkpoint 5, an Interpretive Panel, and rises above the partially-submerged quarry cliffs of Belling Crag. Emerge left, i.e. north-north-west, on to a wide forest road, the North Haul road, a major forest road spanning the entire north shore, and at the 11 mile/17.6 km point (GR.693893) search diligently for a waymark on the left, leading into the spruce and descending north-west to a footbridge crossing the mouth of Belling Burn (GR.690897).

Cross and turn left on to a narrow but distinct path winding south to the wooded peninsula of Cock Stoor, bearing Checkpoint 6. The route winds tortuously through continuous conifer, scrub and tussock, then around the huge promontory of Wind Hill to Checkpoint 7 by Plashetts Quarry, Plashetts Incline and Checkpoint 8, near the site of Plashetts Farm, before emerging on to a forest road at the 17 mile/27.2 km mark (GR.660913).

Plashetts Quarry, a whinstone source for the dam; Plashetts Incline, an inclined railtrack, where tubs of hard-won coal from Plashetts colliery, opened in 1773, descended to a depot on the now submerged Counties Line. In 1911, when coal production reached a peak of 100,000 tons per year, pollution was so heavy the company was sued by a local farmer for loss of crops and animals; he won the case and settled for £83-17s-0d plus 12 guineas costs. Plashetts Coal & Coke Co Ltd was wound up in 1934, the private mine in 1964. For those who master this lonely north shore it is a visual delight, providing sights of water, fell and wildlife rarely seen by the casual stroller, though keep a wary eye out for adders.

Continue north-west along a forest road for nearly 2 miles/3.2 km, passing Gowanburn and Bakethin Weir before descending south at the Otterprint waymark, to the now grassy trackbed of the old Counties Railway, leading to the "Skew-Arched" Viaduct. Descend right, prior to the viaduct, on a stepped path passing an Interpretive

Panel before Checkpoint 9. At the tarmac road descend north to Butteryhaugh Bridge and Bakethin Car Park below the redundant rail track. Rejoin the tree-lined waymarked Counties Line from the car park and continue north-west on to a minor road leading to the C200. Follow the Otterprints south-east along the C200 road for 1½ miles/ 2.4 km to a signpost ("Bakethin Weir"). Plans are afoot to develop a new path through the conservation area by the bird hide, rejoining at Bakethin Weir.

You have now completed 22 miles/35.2 km. Veer left and then right to Checkpoint 10 before rejoining the C200 at Lewis Burn Bridge. Go over the bridge and then left to Matthews Linn Car Park and Toilets, before plunging through banks of willow herb, a precursor for a wild, midge-infested stretch winding south and east to the peninsula of Hawkhirst and Checkpoint 11. This mull is much favoured by the scouting movement, from whose southern tip Checkpoint 12 can be seen a mere 200yds away, across the inlet. Our wooded path circumnavigates the inky darkness of the still water, west and south-east for 1 mile/1.6 km, to reach Checkpoint 12 and commence the final winding mile through a pasture field, complete, I fear, with a sometime resident bull.

Cross the last of the footbridges into Leaplish Waterside Park for the remaining triumphant yards to clock-in and crash-out at Leaplish Lodge; above which reiving Scots left another bloody trail by what is now Leaplish Barn.

[NOTE: Northumbrian Water Limited reserve the right, in the interests of the walker, to make any minor route changes they deem necessary.]

GLOSSARY

LOCAL TERMS & NAMES

Abydings Houses (medieval)
Auld Old
Bastle Fortified farmhouse, defensive
Blake A common or public place
Blaw Blow or puff
Bonnie Dundee, Graham of Claverhouse Loyalist commander and scourge of the covenanters
Brig Bridge
Burn Hill stream
Cadger Itinerant hawker or carter
Cairn Pile of stones, marking a burial chamber, boundary or a route
Capstone Single stone slab covering a cist or burial chamber - Bronze & Iron Age
Caste doune Thrown down
Cauld Weir or Salmon leap. Border Scots - cold
Chatter/Fillers Small stone/rubble packing the centre of a drystone dyke
Cist Stone coffin or a box
Clarty Muddy
Cleugh Secluded gully with a burn
Crag/Craig Rocky outcrop or cliff
Crowdy A mixture of oatmeal and warm water
Currick Sheep shelter, cairn, pile of stones
Dean/Dene Picturesque small gorge with watercourse
Dolmen Stone table, stone slab with two stone uprights
Decaie Decay or degeneration (medieval)
Dinmond(t) 2nd year male sheep
Drift A mine, tunnelled into a seam in the hillside
Drover Man who drove (walked) cattle to the markets
Dyke A drystone wall
Feral Animals once domesticated now living wild
Flow Upland mires, receiving their water from atmosphere
Hag A gully of naked peat, invariably glutinous
Haugh A flat field by a watercourse
Heid Head
Hope A sheltered valley

Knowe Small hill/hillock
KWCCW Kielder Water Circuit Challenge Walk
Linn Waterfall
Long House 18th century single-storey farmhouse, for man and his animals
Lumb Chimney
Mart Livestock or Cattle Market
Mire/Moss An extremely wet peat bog, often the source of a burn
Moss-trooper Families who reived through the Border mires
Mull Peninsula
Nolt Cattle
Nae No
Pele Fortified tower, defensive, of the "family" chief
Raptor Bird of prey with a curved beak and claws
Reiver Cattle thief/blackmailer or freedom fighter?
Resetter Receiver of stolen goods, or fence
Ride Fire break or division between stands of conifers
Rigg Ridge or shoulder of high ground
Robbing Holes Entry into burial cairns by grave robbers
Sae So
Shieling A primitive high-level summer stone shelter.
Siclike Such like
Sike/Syke Small burn or stream
Skew Angled or twisted
Smale Smuggler
Smoot Small opening, at ground level, in a drystone dyke for sheep
Spang Spun or bounced
Spate Flood or torrent
Stand A block or section of planted conifers
Stane Stone
Steading Farm buildings around farmhouse
Stell A stone sheep shelter on the fell fringes; (old term for pen)
Stelling Penning sheep
Thruft A through stone, binding a drystone wall
Toll A charge or levy
Tub Small wheeled container carrying coal from the face
Wether A castrated ram/tup

BIBLIOGRAPHY

The Alternative Pennine Way, Denis Brooke & Phil Hinchcliffe, Cicerone Press, 1992.

The Border Country: A Walker's Guide, Alan Hall, Cicerone Press, 1993.

The Border Line, James Logan Mack, 1930.

Border Pubs & Inns: A Walker's Guide, Alan Hall, Cicerone Press, 1994.

The Borders, F R Banks, B T Batsford Ltd, 1977.

Classic Walks in the Pennines, Terry Marsh, Sigma Press, 1994.

Highways and Byways in the Border, Andrew and John Lang, MacMillan and Co., 1913.

The Kielder Forests, a Forestry Commission Guide, Keith Wilson, Scott Leathart (Eds.), 1982.

The North British Railway in Northumberland, G W M Sewell, Merlin Books, 1990.

Ride with the Moonlight, Michael J H Robson, Liddesdale Heritage Association, 1990.

The Steel Bonnets, George MacDonald Fraser, Barrie & Jenkins 1971, & Collins 1989 (pbk).

Upper North Tynedale, Beryl Charlton, Northumbrian Water, 1987.

Walks in Reiver Country, A Northumberland National Park Publication, 1994.

USEFUL INFORMATION

Accommodation - Details and booking service from Tourist Information Offices and Centres.

County Archaeologist, Northumberland County Council, County Hall, Morpeth, Northumberland NE61 2EF. Tel: (01670) 533000. Fax: (01670) 533253.

Forestry Commission, Headquarters, 231 Corstorphine Road, Edinburgh EH12 7AT. Tel: (0131) 334 0303.

> *Environmental Officer*, Forest Enterprise, Eals Burn, Bellingham Hexham, Northumberland NE48 2AJ. Tel: (01434) 220242. Fax: (01434) 220756.
>
> *Backpacking Sites*, Recreation Forester, Kielder District, Forest Enterprise, Eals Burn, Bellingham, Hexham NE48 2AJ. Tel: (01434) 220242. Fax: (01434) 220242.

Kielder Castle Visitor Centre, Kielder, Bellingham, Northumberland. Tel: (01434) 250209. Open every day from 24 March to 31 October; winter months Saturday and Sunday only, 11am-4pm.

Northumberland National Park, Recreation & Visitor Services, Eastburn, South Park, Hexham, Northumberland NE46 1BS. Tel: (01434) 605555. Fax: (01434) 600522.

Northumbria Tourist Board, Head Office, Aykley Heads, Durham DH1 5UX. Tel: (0191) 384 6905. Fax: (0191) 386 0899.

> *Tourist Information Centre*, Tower Knowe, Kielder Water, Falstone, Hexham, Northumberland. Tel: (01434) 240398.
>
> *Tourist Information Centre*, Main Street, Bellingham, Hexham NE48 2BH. Tel: (01434) 220616.

Northumbrian Water Ltd., Head Office, Abbey Road, Pity Me, Durham DH1 5FJ. Tel: (0191) 383 2222. Fax: (0191) 384 1920.

> *Recreation & Conservation Officer*, as Head Office above.
>
> *Kielder Water Visitor Centre*, Tower Knowe, Falstone, Hexham, Northumberland NE48 1BX. Tel: (01434) 240398. Open all year.
>
> *Leaplish Waterside Park*, Kielder Water, Falstone, Hexham, Northumberland NE48 1BX. Tel: (01434) 250312 for MV Osprey ferry bookings.

Rescue Services/Police - Freephone Dial 999.

Rights of Way, Northumberland County Council, County Hall, Morpeth, Northumberland NE61 2EF. Tel: (01670) 534084.

Scottish Borders Tourist Board, Information Centre, Murrays Green, Jedburgh, Roxburghshire TD8 6BE. Tel: (01835) 863688. Open all year.

Youth Hostels Association, Head Office, Trevelyan House, St Albans, Hertfordshire AL1 2DY. Tel: (01727) 55215.

Byrness Hostel, 18 South Green, Byrness. Tel: (01830) 20222. Open March-September.

Weather Forecasts, Newcastle Meteorological Office, Newcastle

Weather Centre, for North Tynedale and Cheviots. Tel: (0191) 232 6453.

Weather Call, 7 day regional forecast: NE England (01891) 112261. Scottish Borders (01891) 112260.

Metro Radio, daily forecast: FM 97.1, AM 1152.

Radio Newcastle, daily forecast: FM 95.4 & 96.0, AM 1458.

Radio Borders, daily forecast: FM 96.8.

Tyne Tees Television, daily forecast: Channel 3 and Teletext page 183.

Weather Watchers, any area: Tel: (016445) 652 422.

Radio Wavelengths and Teletext page number correct at the time of publication.

Designated in 1956, Northumberland National Park is one of eleven National Parks in England and Wales. Within its boundary, which stretches from the Scottish border south to Hadrian's Wall, lie 1,030 square kilometres of wild and lonely hills, remote valleys and windswept moors. The land is mostly in private ownership and National Park designation does not confer any additional rights of public access.

The National Park has three centres providing exhibitions, video presentations, information and sales of books, maps and souvenirs:
Once Brewed (01434 3444396), on the B6318 near Hadrian's Wall; Rothbury (01669 620887) in Coquetdale, and Ingram (01665 578248) in the Breamish Valley. The centres are open daily between Easter and Autumn. National Park Information Points are located in retail outlets in several villages in and around the Park.

A bumper programme of guided walks, events and activities is organised throughout the year, and two books describing walks in the National Park, **Walks in Reiver Country** and **Walks in High Hills Country** are available from centres and outlets.

For further information please contact:
Northumberland National Park, Eastburn, South Park, HEXHAM NE46 1BS Tel (01434) 605555.

Questa Publishing

Established in 1994, Questa Publishing specialise in producing small, pocket-sized walking guidebooks intended for use by walkers at all standards. Two series of books are currently available:

WALKS WITH CHILDREN, which aim to encourage children to take to the hills and the countryside, and provide them with challenging, but enjoyable, walks, quite often to the summits of mountain, by carefully chosen routes.

Walks with Children in the Lake district:
Patterdale
Buttermere and the Vale of Lorton
Borrowdale
Around Coniston

Walks with Children in the Surrey Hills

Walks with Children in the Yorkshire Dales:
Wensleydale and Swaledale
Wharfedale

In the COUNTRY WALKS series, attention is directed towards the weekend and occasional walker, as well as those who come to walking for the first time. The walks generally range in length from 1½ miles up to 13, and the detailed route descriptions are interwoven with points of interest and historical note.

Kielder Country Walks
Brontë Country Walks
Country Walks are Keswick
Country Walks around Kendal

Books are available from bookshops, or direct from QUESTA PUBLISHING, 27 CAMWOOD, CLAYTON GREEN, BAMBER BRIDGE, PRESTON, PR5 8LA